AMERICAN ECONOMIC HISTORY ★ A Garland Series

Edited by
STUART BRUCHEY
Columbia University

COSTS OF CONTRACTING AND THE DECLINE OF TENANCY IN THE SOUTH, 1930-1960

Lee J. Alston

Garland Publishing, Inc.
New York & London ★ 1985

Library of Congress Cataloging in Publication Data

Alston, Lee J., 1951–
Costs of contracting and the decline of tenancy in the South, 1930–1960.

(American economic history)
Originally presented as the author's thesis (doctoral—University of Washington, 1978.)
Bibliography: p.
1. Farm tenancy—Southern States—History—20th century. 2. Agricultural wages—Southern States—History—20th century. 3. Agriculture—Southern States—Costs—History—20th century. 4. Southern States—Race relations. I. Title. II. Series.
HD1511.U6A133 1985 333.5′3′0975 84-48302
ISBN 0-8240-6650-2

All volumes in this series are printed on acid-free, 250-year-life paper.
Printed in the United States of America

Costs of Contracting and the Decline of Tenancy in the South, 1930-1960

by

Lee J. Alston

A dissertation submitted in partial fulfillment of the requirements for the degree of

Doctor of Philosophy

University of Washington

1978

FOREWORD

This work was completed in 1978. Parts of the manuscript have since been published, but there is merit in having the theoretical and empirical analysis appear in its entirety. Subsequent research by myself and others has clarified and extended some of my theoretical arguments yet I believe it is fair to say that the recent work is consistent with the theories, methods and conclusions presented here.

Lee J. Alston
Williamstown, Massachusetts
August 1984

Table of Contents

List of Figures

List of Tables

Acknowledgements

I would like to thank the members of my dissertation committee, Vernon Carstensen, Douglass North, Richard Parks and Potluri Rao, for their comments and assistance. I acknowledge a special debt to Mary, my wife, for her editing, encouragement and support, and to Robert Higgs, my dissertation chairman, for his ideas, advice, and friendship.

Introduction

The Historical Facts at Issue

Between 1930 and 1960 the agricultural labor force in the South declined from 39 percent of the total labor force to 8.6 percent.[1] Both the number of tenants and the number of wage workers fell during the same period; however, the decline was much greater in the number of tenants than in the number of wage workers.[2] The ratio of the number of tenants to real wages paid fell from 0.0141 to 0.00018.[3] Most of the literature dealing with the decline of tenancy in the twentieth century explains the decline in the absolute number of tenant contracts[4] but does not clearly delineate between factors that account for the absolute decline in agricultural workers and those that caused a decline in tenant contracts relative to wage contracts. In

---

[1] Joseph D. Reid, Jr., "Sharecropping and Tenancy in American History" (October 1976), forthcoming in James Roumasset, ed., *Risk and Uncertainty in Agriculture* (University of California Press), p. 36.

[2] Ibid., p. 41.

[3] Real wages paid is a better proxy for wage contracts than the number of hired laborers because "persons hired" gives no indication of the number of hours of labor services provided by each worker.

[4] Moses S. Musoke, "Technical Change in Cotton Production in the U.S., 1925-1960" (unpublished Ph.D. dissertation, University of Wisconsin-Madison, 1976).

this thesis, I focus on developing a model to account for the relative decline in tenant contracts from 1930 to 1960 in ten Southern states. The states considered are North Carolina, South Carolina, Georgia, Tennessee, Alabama, Mississippi, Arkansas, Louisiana, Oklahoma and Texas. The decline in the ratio of average number of tenants to real wages paid per county in agriculture for each state for the census years 1930, 1940, 1945, 1950, 1955 and 1960 is shown in Table 1.

In 1930 there was a large variation among the states in the absolute number of tenants, in real wages paid and in the ratio of tenants to real wages. In Mississippi, where the ratio of tenants to real wages was the highest (0.0316), the average number of tenants per county was 2,761 while the average real wages paid per county were $87,320. The lowest ratio of tenants to real wages was in Texas, which had an average of 1,103 tenants and an average wage payment of $247,480 per county. The median ratio of tenants to real wages (0.0131) was in North Carolina, where the corresponding numbers for tenants and real wages were 1,251 and $95,517. By 1960 there was little absolute difference across states in the ratio of tenants to real wages. The range was from 0.00030 in Alabama to 0.00005 in Texas. The corresponding absolute numbers were 333 tenants per county in Alabama to 209 tenants per county in Texas and

Table 1

Ratio of the Number of Tenants to Real Wages over Time and across States

State	Number of Tenants/Real Wages Paid 1930	1940	1945	1950	1955	1960
NC	0.0131	0.0127	0.0018	0.0010	0.0007	0.0002
SC	0.0108	0.0100	0.0020	0.0010	0.0006	0.0002
GA	0.0153	0.0118	0.0025	0.0010	0.0005	0.0002
TE	0.0101	0.0123	0.0019	0.0008	0.0006	0.0003
AL	0.0279	0.0278	0.0474	0.0017	0.0008	0.0002
MI	0.0316	0.0283	0.0035	0.0011	0.0007	0.0001
AR	0.0164	0.0167	0.0017	0.0006	0.0004	0.0001
LO	0.0050	0.0053	0.0007	0.0004	0.0003	0.0001
OK	0.0065	0.0130	0.0013	0.0005	0.0004	0.0002
TX	0.0045	0.0051	0.0005	0.0002	0.0001	0.00005

Source: See Appendix A.

$1,105,669 in real wages paid per county in Alabama to $3,813,675 in real wages paid in Texas.

Plan of the Study

Before developing and testing my model, I will review the literature that discusses the demise of tenancy in the twentieth century South and the literature in which economic theories of risk and transactions costs are applied to the problem of contractual choice (Chapter 1). After formally presenting (Chapter 2) and testing (Chapter 3) the hypotheses derived from my model, I will discuss the impact of the relative rise in wage contracts on race relations in the rural plantation South (Chapter 4).

Chapter 1

A Review of the Tenancy Literature

Theoretical Studies

Until recently, interest in share contracting and tenancy has varied directly with changes in the percentage of farms operated by tenants. After 1930, tenancy declined and began to lose the attention of economists and policy-makers. Within the past decade there has been a renewed interest in the theoretical aspects of agricultural labor contracts. In this section, I will review the contributions of Steven N.S. Cheung, Joseph D. Reid, David M.G. Newberry, Joseph E. Stiglitz and Robert Higgs.[1] Except for Higgs, all of these authors attempt to explain the existence of share contracting; Higgs's aim is to account for changes in the mix of contracts across time

---

[1] Steven N.S. Cheung, _The Theory of Share Tenancy_ (Chicago, University of Chicago Press, 1969), and "Transactions Costs, Risk Aversion, and the Choice of Contractual Arrangements," _Journal of Law and Economics_, XII (April 1969), 23-42; Robert Higgs, "Race, Tenure and Resource Allocation in Southern Agriculture, 1910," _Journal of Economic History_, XXXIII (March 1973), 146-69, and "Patterns of Farm Rental in the Georgia Cotton Belt," _Journal of Economic History_, XXXIV (June 1964), 468-82; David M.G. Newberry, "Sharecropping and Uncertain Labor Markets," _Review of Economic Studies_, 44 (October 1977), 585-94; Joseph D. Reid, "Sharecropping as an Understandable Market Response--The Postbellum South," _Journal of Economic History_, XXXIII (March 1973), 106-30; Joseph E. Stiglitz, "Incentives and Risk Sharing in Sharecropping," _Review of Economic Studies_, 61 (April 1974), 219-56.

and among regions. The model developed in Chapter 2 is based in part on the theories set forth in these studies.

Steven N.S. Cheung should be credited with sparking the revival of share contracting as a topic of research. Cheung examines the costs and benefits of adopting fixed rent contracts versus share contracts and attempts to refute the proposition that share contracting is inefficient.[2] Under an efficient contract, labor expends services until its marginal product (which under a share contract is divided between landlord and worker) is just equal to its opportunity cost (the prevailing wage). Inefficiency arises under a share contract because a worker stops supplying labor when his share of the additional output just equals his opportunity cost. Theoretically, both parties could increase their income by switching from a share to a fixed rent contract; therefore, if there were no other compensating benefits associated with share contracts, they would never exist.

---

[2] Several studies by economists in the U.S. Department of Agriculture pointed out the beneficial aspects of share contracts: U.S. Department of Agriculture, "Relation of Land Tenure to Plantation Organization," by C.O. Brannen, Bulletin No. 1269 (Washington, D.C.: Government Printing Office, 1924); U.S. Department of Agriculture, Yearbook of Agriculture, 1923, "Farm Ownership and Tenancy," by L.C. Gray and others (Washington, D.C.: Government Printing Office, 1924). For additional contemporary studies that addressed sharecropping as an efficient system, see the citations in Higgs, "Race, Tenure and Resource Allocation in Southern Agriculture, 1910," p. 152, footnotes 5-6.

Cheung questions how an apparently inefficient system of agriculture could persist for centuries. He maintains that because landlords and tenants are risk averse, both can gain by adopting a share contract that distributes risk between them. However, share contracting must entail offsetting costs; otherwise we would never observe any fixed rent contracts. Under a share contract, transactions costs are increased by the necessity of monitoring the input and output of labor to insure that the terms of the contract are met. Whether or not a share contract is chosen will depend upon weighing the gains from risk dispersal against the transactions costs of negotiation, supervision and enforcement. Differences in transactions costs and varying degrees of risk aversion among individuals account for the existence of share contracts as well as for why they are not used exclusively.

Although Cheung recognizes the crucial differences (with respect to risk-bearing and transactions costs) between fixed rent and share contracts, his analysis is nevertheless flawed. He focuses on the risk dispersal gains obtained by shifting to a share contract from a fixed rent contract but he ignores the costs. Under a fixed rent contract, risk is borne entirely by the tenant; under a share contract, its incidence varies according to each party's claim to the output. The tenant gains by shifting from a fixed rent to a share contract, but the landlord, if he is also risk averse, loses because he now bears some risk previously borne by the tenant. Unless compensated for this additional risk bearing, landlords have no incentive to adopt a share contract.

By neglecting to consider fixed wage as a possible contractual choice, Cheung did not recognize the positive role share contracts play in reducing transactions costs. Under a fixed wage contract, a worker's remuneration is not dependent upon total output and therefore labor has no incentive to increase output. By switching from a fixed wage to a share contract, labor has an incentive to increase output because labor's compensation is now a function of output.

While Cheung's model provides an explanation for the existence of share contracting, it does not provide any theory from which refutable hypotheses can be derived. Cheung states that:

> Two factors appear to be important in explaining different patterns of contractual choices in different localities. First, different physical attributes of crops and types of climates often result in different variances of outputs in different agricultural areas. Second, different legal arrangements . . . affect the variances of income as well as affecting transactions costs for the contracting parties.[3]

---

[3] Cheung, "Transaction Costs, Risk Aversion, and the

More specific causal relationships must be formulated before Cheung's model can be utilized by an empirical scientist. It is true that different crops have different price and output risks associated with them, but Cheung's model supplies no prediction of the change in contractual mix in response to changes in the level of risk. In addition, by ignoring the possibility of fixed wage contracts, Cheung's model would lead us erroneously to predict that as transactions costs rise, the absolute number of share contracts would fall. In order to make such a prediction, we need to be able to measure the impact of rising transactions costs on all three possible agricultural contracts. All one is able to predict *a priori* is that the contracts under which transactions costs are greatest (fixed wage) would fall and the contracts under which transactions costs are the least (fixed rental) would rise. The impact on share contracts is ambiguous because parties have an incentive to shift from share to fixed rent contracts. (The relative costs associated with each contract will be explained in Chapter 2.)

Joseph Reid's rationale for the existence of sharecropping is that it reduces risk rather than disperses it as in Cheung's model. According to Reid, output risk is

---

Choice of Contractual Arrangements," pp. 29-30.

smaller under share contracts than under fixed wage or fixed rent contracts. The costs of renegotiating the share contract in order to minimize the vagaries associated with agricultural production are less than with either fixed rent or fixed wage contracts:

> A major impetus for the coexistence of renting, sharecropping and owner cultivation with fixed wage labor may be sharecropping's lower transaction costs over the life of the contract. Agricultural production and deviation from expectation occur over the growing season. . . . As deviation from the prior expectation increased, so would the profitability of contract renegotiation between the landlord and tenant. For example, if unexpectedly favorable weather over the first part of the growing season increased anticipated yield, the profitability of more intensive cultivation of the enhanced crops--to the neglect of the less favored crops and negotiated land maintenance or improved duties--would rise. To efficiently take advantage of this unexpected situation, contractual renegotiation is required. . . .
>
> . . . .
>
> The central feature of a sharecropping contract is the continuing interest of both landlord and tenant in the efficiency of agricultural production.[4]

Contrary to Reid's assertions, the party or parties who are bearing all of the risk would have an incentive to farm efficiently regardless of the type of contract. Efficiency, however, does not necessarily require renegotiation under all contracts. Certain adjustments may be

---

[4] Reid, *op. cit.*, pp. 125-26.

possible without any renegotiation under a fixed rent or fixed wage contract. Provided that a fixed renter can still meet all of the terms of the contract, he could farm more intensively (adjusting his leisure, hiring wage labor or enlisting family help) and reap the entire gain from the favorable conditions. Since the fixed renter agreed to bear the entire output risk, he most likely believes that he could marginally adjust to reap the rewards from output uncertainty. Similarly, renegotiation need not transpire under fixed wage contracts. To take advantage of favorable output conditions, a landlord could either reassign his present wage force (switching labor from cultivation of corn to cotton or from building fences to cultivation) or hire more labor from off the farm. If labor markets are tight, wages have to be increased to secure more workers, but this does not entail renegotiation over claims to the windfall in output.

Under either a fixed wage or fixed rent contract no renegotiation costs occur because only one party has a claim to the output. Under a share contract each party has a claim to part of the final output. If a difference of opinion arises as to how to adjust inputs in response to changes in the weather, the potential gains from adjustment could be dissipated in settling the dispute. Precisely because each party has something at stake if a misadjustment occurs, arguments are likely to arise. As J.R. Godwin, a Tennessee planter, explained:

> You mix up less with the people when you rent the land than on shares. If you rent on the share system, you undertake a supervision of cultivating the crop and you watch how they are managing it; they feel as if they are going to make a good crop and ought not to be interfered with, and you feel they are not doing it just to suit you. You are more likely to get up friction on either side than when you rent the land and they know just what they have to pay and you know what to expect. All you know about is to see that they do not abuse your land and allow it to wash away, and that is a small thing.[5]

Reid presents no empirical evidence to substantiate his claim that risk is reduced through renegotiation of contracts. Perhaps there is little that can be altered in response to changes in prior expectations, or perhaps those marginal adjustments that can be made (e.g., more intensive weeding) can best be accomplished if no renegotiation takes place. Even though renegotiation may take place under a share contract, the costs of settling a difference of opinion may be greater than the efficiency gains.

In Reid's model the full continuum of contracts is explained by differences in the skill and managerial ability of landlords and tenants. The greater the

---

[5] Cited in Higgs, "Patterns of Farm Rental in the Georgia Cotton Belt, 1880-1900," p. 477.

managerial ability of landlords and the less skilled a tenant, the greater are the gains from renegotiation; therefore, we ought to observe more share contracts relative to fixed rent contracts. Reid hypothesizes that, "As the managerial complexity of the crop increases (from the possibility of fruitfully applying fertilizer, for example), sharecropping should become increasingly preferred."[6] Unfortunately, Reid does not present any test of his hypothesis. Technical change, such as tractor adoption, could change the managerial complexity of farming and, since technical change is an integral part of my theory, I plan to test its impact upon tenancy and thereby indirectly test Reid's hypothesis.

David Newberry is primarily concerned with deriving the mathematical conditions under which share contracting is and is not efficient. The risk dispersal and risk reduction properties of contracts are examined. He demonstrates that the same distribution of risk associated with a share contract can be achieved by landlords and tenants provided that fixed rent and fixed wage contracts can be costlessly combined. Therefore, assuming that share contracts entail more supervision costs than either fixed wage or fixed rent contracts, share contracts are inefficient.

---

[6] Reid, op. cit., p. 126.

The analysis is flawed by Newberry's failure to specify correctly the transactions costs associated with the three contractual forms. In fact, transactions costs are lowest under fixed rent and greatest under fixed wage contracts. The disincentive effects associated with a share contract might not be greater than those associated with a combination of contracts. In addition, it seems reasonable to assume that the costs of negotiation with two contracts combined exceed those where only one share contract is adopted.

Newberry derives the above results by assuming constant returns to scale. He demonstrates that, if there are output economies of scale, sharecropping offers risk dispersal advantages over a combination of fixed rent and wage contracts. In order to attain the same distribution of risk for a given acreage share contracted, it would be necessary to combine two smaller units, one under a fixed rental and the other under a fixed wage contract. Under either a fixed rental or fixed wage contract, production units would be smaller (for any given distribution of risk) and output per acre would be less. If new technology introduces economies of scale, then we should observe more share contracting with technological adoption. This is an interesting testable hypothesis if it can be demonstrated that economies of scale are different under different technologies.

Newberry maintains that share contracts are essential for efficiency because they reduce the risk associated with labor markets. Labor risks are of two types, uncertainty of employment and unpredictable wages. By unpredictable wages, Newberry is referring to uncertainty surrounding the purchasing power of wages. He maintains that paying labor in kind, which is customary under most share contracts, reduces the risk from price uncertainty. This rationale alone could not justify share contracting because payments in kind can be made under fixed rent or fixed wage contracts. In addition, in-kind payments reduce wage risk only if the variance in the purchasing power of money wages exceeds the variance in crop prices. Normally one would expect less variance in a weighted sum of prices (CPI) than in a single crop price and therefore less risk associated with money payments than with in-kind payments.

Newberry maintains that employment risk can be reduced through either a share contract or a fixed wage contract but not with a fixed rent contract. For this reason, a combination of fixed rent and fixed wage contracts would not offer the same advantages as a single share contract. By employment risk, Newberry is referring to the uncertainty of securing employment throughout the year. Employment risk is eliminated under a share or fixed wage contract by a yearly contract; however, under a fixed rental, Newberry maintains that risk is increased by a yearly guarantee of employment. His argument is as follows:

> The existence of one year labour contracts might seem to solve the problem, but they do not allow fixed rent tenants the kind of riskless labour contracts they need. The amount of labour to be supplied on a one year labour contract has to be specified in advance, before the tenant knows how much labour he wants to buy or sell at each stage of production. Marginal adjustments to labour inputs can be made only through the risky casual labour market. Indeed, creating some permanent labour will tend to increase the riskiness of the casual labour market, and may not improve the overall risk-sharing opportunities available to the economy.[7]

Newberry appears to be intermingling the employment uncertainty faced by employees with that faced by employers. Risk for the two parties moves in opposite directions. When analyzing fixed wage and share contracts, Newberry examines only the risk faced by employees, but when considering fixed rent contracts, where the tenant is also an employer, he addresses employment uncertainty faced by employers. Employment uncertainty for a tenant (as an employee) is eliminated by a permanent contract. Employment uncertainty for a fixed renter (as an employer of additional labor) can also be eliminated by hiring permanent laborers at the outset of the season. Uncertainty of employment from an

---

[7] Newberry, op. cit., p. 586.

employer's and an employee's point of view is invariant with respect to the type of contract.

Joseph Stiglitz examines both the risk dispersal and the incentive attributes of share contracting. He finds, as does Newberry, that there are no additional risk dispersal benefits from share contracting if workers and landlords can costlessly mix contracts, if the production function is characterized by constant returns to scale and if enforcement costs are zero.

Stiglitz explains the existence of share contracting by relaxing the assumption of zero enforcement costs:

> The sharecropping system is adopted because of its incentive effects (when direct supervision is costly or ineffective) and because of its risk-sharing features. Although the rental system has greater incentive effects, it forces the worker to bear all the risks, and although the wage system allows the landlord, if he is risk neutral, to absorb all the risk, it may force heavy supervision costs on him.[8]

The implication of this analysis is that only share contracting should exist. In order to explain a continuum of contracts, it is necessary to assume different preferences on the part of landlords and tenants towards risk and supervision.

Stiglitz's major contribution for my purposes is his

Stiglitz, op. cit., p. 251.

description of how supervision costs associated with different contracts are affected by the introduction of capital. The owner of the new capital has an incentive to monitor its use. If labor and capital are employed together (e.g., man and tractor), the marginal costs of supervising labor (assuming one is already supervising capital) fall. It is clear, as Stiglitz reasons, that if capital is owned by the landlord, the desirability of a wage contract increases, but it would not necessarily follow, as he asserts, that if capital is owned by the worker, a fixed rental would be preferred. Unless the introduction of capital by workers changes the costs of supervising labor, the landowner has no incentive to change contractual form. The worker will have an incentive to monitor his capital irrespective of the contract, but this does not affect the labor supervision costs of the landowner. The introduction of new farming techniques, Stiglitz maintains, produces results similar to the introduction of capital. Because a landlord needs to supervise the implementation of new technology, the additional costs of supervising labor inputs fall, and as supervision costs for labor fall we expect the relative number of wage contracts to rise.

The introduction of capital into a world with only land and labor would most likely lower supervision costs per unit of labor as Stiglitz describes, but this result does not necessarily imply that the introduction of more capital requires more monitoring. Certain new techniques, more capital intensive than the old, may actually lower the supervision costs of both labor and capital. For example, it may be easier to monitor the marginal product of capital and the marginal product of labor when using tractor techniques than it is when using mule techniques. The impact of technical change will be discussed when I specify my model. Nevertheless, I agree with Stiglitz's conclusion that as supervision costs per unit of labor fall, we should observe more wage contracts.

Risk dispersal coupled with the presence of transactions costs can account for the simultaneous existence of fixed rent, share and fixed wage contracts, but none of the models presented so far can answer the question of which contract will be preferred when the absolute amount of output risk in agriculture increases. Robert Higgs provides an answer and also points out where other models are deficient:

> The difficulty is that if both the landlord and the tenant are averse to risk, then each will wish to shift risk onto the other as the level of risk increases; these tendencies are mutually inconsistent and no mechanism is provided for reconciling them.[9]

---

[9] Higgs, "Race, Tenure and Resource Allocation in Southern Agriculture, 1910," p. 153.

Higgs assumes that although individuals differ in their behavior toward risk, as a class agricultural workers are relatively more risk averse than landowners, because they are less wealthy and have less access to credit markets. This assumption allows Higgs to predict that as the level of risk rises, the number of share contracts relative to fixed rentals increases because workers are willing to pay a relatively higher price than landlords to avoid the increase in risk. Higgs tests this hypothesis with data for 1910 and the results support his hypothesis. I intend to conduct a similar test using data for the period 1930-1960.

Higgs also specifies causal factors that account for differences in supervision costs across farms and therefore influence contractual choice. By considering the influence of farm size, his model explains the existence of a mix of contracts as well as predicting the direction of preferred contractual choice. Total supervision costs increase with farm size simply because there are more people to monitor. Because tenant contracts reduce supervision costs relative to wage contracts, there exists a positive relationship between farm size and tenant contracts. Higgs's hypothesis is supported by tests using data from the period 1880-1900 in the Georgia cotton belt. An implicit assumption in Higgs's model is that all sizes of farms utilize the same technology in crop production.

Although a realistic assumption for the time period he considered, it is not for the period 1930-1960. An integral part of my model is the explanation of how different cotton techniques affect supervision costs and in turn influence contractual choice.

Empirical Studies

In developing my model of tenancy, I have relied on previous empirical studies of the causes of the decline in tenancy. Scholars who have examined this issue include Richard Day, Moses Musoke, John Fulmer, Anthony Tang, James Street and C.O. Brannen.[10] The main features of their papers are discussed in this section.

Richard Day designs a linear programming model to generate estimates of production, investment, and the utilization of land and labor in Southern agriculture. The

---

[10] U.S. Department of Agriculture, "Relation of Land Tenure to Plantation Organization," by C.O. Brannen, Bulletin No. 1269 (Washington, D.C.: Government Printing Office, 1924); Richard Day, "Technological Change and the Sharecropper," *American Economic Review*, LVII (June 1967), 427-449; John L. Fulmer, *Agricultural Progress in the Cotton Belt Since 1920* (Chapel Hill: University of North Carolina Press, 1950); Moses S. Musoke, "Technical Change in Cotton Production in the U.S., 1925-60" (unpublished Ph.D. dissertation, University of Wisconsin-Madison, 1976); James H. Street, *The New Revolution in the Cotton Economy* (Chapel Hill: University of North Carolina Press, 1957); Anthony Tang, *Economic Development in the Southern Piedmont, 1860-1950* (Chapel Hill: University of North Carolina Press, 1958).

shift into various techniques (from mule and manpower alone to complete mechanization) is viewed as the outcome of decisions by profit-maximizing individuals. The test area for his model is the Mississippi Delta, and the time period considered is 1940-58. Throughout this period there was a trend toward lower total labor requirements. In Day's model, labor requirements are affected by changes in machine technology, fertilizer usage and crop mixes. These in turn are determined by the relative prices of inputs (labor and capital) and outputs. For any profit-maximizing target level of output, increased use of either fertilizer or machinery dictates a decline in labor inputs. Similarly, a shift out of cotton into corn, soybeans, or other less labor-intensive crops further reduces labor demand. The various stages of profit-maximizing technical change exert differential impacts on the seasonal demand for labor:

> The consequence of adopting stages II and III (tractor adoption and complete mechanization except for hand picking of cotton) was to eliminate virtually all hand labor except for the summer weeding and fall harvesting seasons. This meant that the maintenance of sharecroppers the year round became uneconomic. Instead a combination of resident wage labor and labor hired from nearby villages was favored.[11]

The implications are not as clear as Day suggests.

---

[11] Day, *op. cit.*, p. 439.

Sharecropping becomes necessarily "uneconomic" only if the total payment to share labor cannot be adjusted. Because the acreage per laborer can be reduced, the percentage of total returns received by the labor force can fall. Fringe benefits (e.g., housing, medical care, garden plots) can also be reduced. Theoretically, it appears that a very large number of margins can be adjusted to make sharecropping labor "economic" from the landowner's point of view. Day views the sharecropping system as an inflexible institution rather than as a contractual form. Day's observation that moving to a more capital-intensive technique entailed a relative decline in share contracts is correct. However, in order to explain and understand this shift, we need a theory of how technical change affects the costs of contracting, which Day does not present.

The most recent work on the displacement of the Southern labor force is that of Moses Musoke. He develops a model based on comparative costs which predicts a shift towards capital. He chooses the comparative cost approach because it permits "two processes to coexist in the same region even if one is more profitable than the other as long as for each method average returns exceed average costs."[12] Non-profit-maximizing behavior is not essential

---

[12] Musoke, _op_. _cit_., p. 94.

to explain the existence of two competing techniques. Another possible, and perhaps more plausible explanation, is that different operators face different costs. Nevertheless, the application of his model to three southern states (Texas, Mississippi, and South Carolina) demonstrates that differences in the relative costs of the mule and tractor techniques can account for differences in the timing of tractor adoption and therefore labor displacement. A crucial assumption in Musoke's model is that the size of the farm is fixed. Operators decide the mix of capital and labor given a specific size farm; the size of the farm, even in the long run, is not subject to adjustment. This assumption gives rise to the predicted lack of investment in relatively "lumpy" capital-intensive innovations in South Carolina and Mississippi. On empirical grounds, this assumption appears invalid for certain sections of the South. For example, in the Mississippi Delta region numerous small farms are owned by one individual who could, if costs warranted it, operate his total contiguous land holdings as one large farm rather than as numerous tenant farms. In cases of large cotton plantations, something other than size must explain the persistence of the mule technique. Musoke correctly argues that the adoption of the tractor had a significant impact on the displacement of labor but, like Day, he does not discuss how adoption of the tractor affected the costs of tenant labor vis-a-vis wage labor.

Musoke also considers how federal farm programs affected Southern cotton farming. The crop restriction program, later supplanted by the soil conservation program, had several important effects on the cotton economy. Because land is only one of several inputs into the production process, a farmer could still increase his other inputs (labor, fertilizer, etc.) so that his output per acre would rise. To the extent that this occurred, the goal of crop restriction was circumvented. Profit-maximizing farmers were induced to produce their output at a higher marginal cost. This does not necessarily mean that farmers in general were worse off with this program because, as long as the demand curve is inelastic in the region considered, total revenue would rise. By restricting the acreage in soil-depleting crops, such as cotton, a relative shift into feed crops and legumes was encouraged. Musoke recognizes that this shift was the effect of the crop restriction program, but the only implication he derives is that the total demand for labor falls. For the purposes of my study, it should be noted that the shift into more feed crops and legumes is associated with a relative rise in wage labor. Changing crop mixes could well have altered the transactions costs of different contractual arrangements.

According to Musoke, the effect of the New Deal farm credit programs was to increase the supply of loanable funds and thereby lower the interest rate. One expects this to have a positive impact on capital formation. Musoke correctly reasons that tractor adoption and therefore labor displacement were fostered, but he does not address the issue of how mechanization might have affected the relative cost of share versus wage labor.

Under the Agricultural Adjustment Act (AAA) benefits program, landlords were required to share the government payments with their tenants. This legal restriction

> threatened to reduce his [the landlord's] net income relative to that of his counterpart who used wage labor. . . . Thus sharing benefit payments, or the threat of its enforcement, tended to raise the shadow wage of the share tenant for the planter. The fact that the AAA administration sought to insure for the share tenant a share that would reflect general improvement in farmers' income made possible by the program created a kind of minimum wage for share labor. Wage labor was not included in AAA efforts and was available at the low market wage that prevailed in the 1930's.[13]

Payments received by tenants were based on the share of the output to which the tenant was entitled. There existed, however, ways in which landlords could circumvent the law

---

[13] _Ibid._, pp. 203-204.

and still retain their share tenants. Considerable evidence indicates that it was not uncommon for tenants never to receive AAA payments:

> It is noted that not all croppers and tenants on participating farms reported having received A.A.A. payments. The complaint has been made from time to time that many croppers and some tenants were deprived of payments due them in accordance with A.A.A. regulations. The findings of this study support this assumption to a limited extent but no data are available for comparison as to whether or not such practices may have been more prevalent prior to 1942.
>
> It should be borne in mind that diversion of payments which were in the nature of farm income, resulted from the relative bargaining position of the landlord and tenant or cropper and is not inherent in the program itself. Such diversion would tend to take place in the same way as the diversion of other returns. There is considerable evidence that the relative bargaining position of the tenant and cropper changes with changing economic conditions and in 1942 was much improved over that in the middle and late thirties.[14]

Unless some institutional rigidities prevented them, numerous adjustments to the share contract could be made so that the real wage paid to share labor remained unaffected. For example, the percentage of the output going to the tenant or the size of the tenant's farm could be reduced. Either would effectively lower labor compensation. James Street lists adjustments that were made without dispensing

---

[14] Harold Hoffsommer, ed., _The Social and Economic Significance of Land Tenure in the Southwestern States_ (Chapel Hill: University of North Carolina Press, 1950), p. 23.

with share contracts:

> A variety of arrangements has been worked out to compensate the operator for increased input costs which formerly were part of the annual contribution of the cropper. Many planters have begun to charge their croppers service fees for the operations performed with power equipment, part of which are used to pay the wages of the tractor driver, who may also be a cropper himself. Others have shifted from the traditional 50-50 to a 60-40 share basis, under which the operator pays for all seed, fertilizer, and poison, and receives in return 60 percent of the crops and 60 percent of the government soil conservation and parity payments.[15]

Because the bargaining strength of labor vis-a-vis landlords was not changed by the AAA requirements, one would expect such behavior to occur. Farm size was the parameter most often changed; it decreased throughout the government payments program even though the percentage of output going to the tenant remained fixed. For example, the average cotton acreage of sharecroppers declined from 14.6 acres in 1932 to 10.5 acres in 1938 on 89 plantations in nine counties in Arkansas.[16] In making adjustments, parties incur certain negotiating costs, but other desirable features of share contracting are retained.

---

[15] Street, _op_. _cit_., p. 219.

[16] Arkansas Agricultural Experiment Station, "Changes in Labor Organization on Cotton Farms," by J.G. McNeely and Glen T. Barton, Bulletin No. 397 (Fayetteville, Arkansas: June 1940), p. 23.

Both Musoke and John Fulmer notice an inverse relationship between cotton yields and sharecropping. When yields rise, the per-acre compensation to labor under a share contract increases. If rising yields are due to any input other than labor, Musoke and Fulmer maintain that landlords have an incentive to shift out of share contracts in order to avoid paying laborers more than the value of their labor services. As previously noted, unless institutional rigidities prevent numerous margins of a share contract from being renegotiated (or the costs of negotiation are prohibitive), we would not necessarily expect a relative decrease in share contracts. For my purposes, the important result of rising cotton yields is that the variance around the mean cotton yield was reduced. Increased fertilizer usage, by restoring nutrients to the soil, not only raised cotton yields but also stabilized yields by reducing the likelihood of a disastrous crop. Consequently, the risk associated with cotton farming declined. When I formulate my hypotheses, I will discuss how a reduction in risk affects the mix of agricultural labor contracts.

James Street's view of the impact of mechanization is similar to that of most scholars; as labor requirements per acre are reduced, the demand for labor will fall. Street's contribution to the problem that I am investigating is his observation that a relative rise in share contracting is associated with labor scarcity.[17] Before Street, C.O. Brannen in a USDA bulletin published in 1924 notes the same behavior.[18] Both Street and Brannen maintain that share contracts prevent labor from leaving the farm before the cotton is harvested. This feature of tenancy becomes more desirable the more difficult it is to find cotton pickers. Theoretically, however, workers could be paid in fixed wages, partially withheld until the crop is harvested, thereby retaining the labor force without altering the other desirable attributes of a fixed wage contract.

A necessary condition for the Street/Brannen hypothesis is that capital markets are imperfect. If a wage earner can secure a loan in order to subsist during the work year, landowners and labor can negotiate a contract withholding a portion of the wage payment (up to 100%). An incentive to remain on the farm is created in this fashion. If the only collateral a worker can offer in return for a loan is his labor services, bankers require a large risk premium which prohibits borrowing by wage earners. Since the landlord has the best information about the creditworthiness of tenants, he is in the best position to make

---

[17] Street, op. cit., pp. 211, 218, 228.

[18] U.S. Department of Agriculture, "Relation of Land Tenure to Plantation Organization," pp. 2, 38.

advances.

As labor markets become tighter, enforcement costs rise under all contractual forms because the opportunity costs (alternative employment possibilities) of the agricultural laborer rise. The incentive to leave the farm before the contract is completed increases as the difference between alternative employment wages and the expected net labor payment (expected labor compensation minus previous living advances) increases. It is essential to the employer that the labor force be adequately fed, clothed and housed during the work year. Under either a delayed fixed wage or a tenant contract, most workers require advances. If these advances are large relative to the expected total payment to labor, there is little incentive to remain through the cotton harvest if alternative employment at higher wages appears (e.g., cotton picking at piece rates or working in factories). Tenant contracts better secure one's labor force only if the expected net payment to a tenant for labor services is higher than the expected net wage payment. Laborers do expect to receive more under tenancy arrangements because they receive a risk premium and require less supervision. The validity of the Street/Brannen argument depends not only on the magnitude of the differential between the expected labor compensations under the two forms of contracting but also on the size of net wage earnings (gross wage payment - advances) relative to alternative earnings. The closer net earnings are to alternative earnings, the more desirable tenancy becomes. In addition, the larger the difference between net expected tenant income and net fixed wage income, the more tenancy we ought to observe when labor markets constrict.

Anthony Tang has studied economic development in the Southern Piedmont region and examined the impact of industrial/urban growth on agriculture. He finds that capital markets improved in localities experiencing urbanization. The appearance of new industrial employment in a locality created greater alternative employment opportunities for agricultural workers, which in turn increased the imputed cost of labor. With the cost of capital falling and the cost of labor rising, a wealth-maximizing landlord would purchase more capital and release labor until the marginal product of labor was equal to the new wage rate. In addition, since it was now easier to obtain credit, Tang reasons that many tenants would purchase their own farms. Tang's logic can account for the absolute decline in the number of tenants, but he does not recognize the impact that increased capital inputs had on the costs of contracting. As I suggested earlier, we expect supervision costs to fall if certain types of capital are adopted; hence, a proportionate rise in wage labor.[19] In Tang's model, tight labor markets ultimately encourage the use of wage contracts via mechanization, whereas in the Street/Brannen model, labor scarcity promotes the use of tenant contracts. The apparent conflict between the two competing hypotheses can be reconciled by differentiating between short- and long-run behavior. Both Tang and Street/Brannen refer to wealth-maximizing responses to changes in labor supply. Tang's hypothesis refers to the long-run adjustments in the farmer's capital/labor ratio, while the Street/Brannen hypothesis pertains to the relatively less costly adjustments that could be made in the short run by adjusting the contractual form. The Street/Brannen hypothesis is more powerful the fewer and less perfect are the available substitutes for labor.

Urbanization, in Tang's model, only influences the absolute number of tenants by inducing a substitution of capital for labor. It also appears, however, that urbanization affects the mix of the remaining contracts. For any given level of employment, the costs associated with labor failing to honor the length of the contract increase the more rural the area. Location near an urban area reduces

---

[19] It may be less costly to monitor the marginal product of capital and the marginal product of labor when using tractor techniques than it is when using mule techniques. The rationale for this assertion will be provided in Chapter 2.

search costs by allowing landlords to draw upon a larger population base. I intend to further specify, in Chapter 2, the link between urbanization and the relative mix of tenant and wage contracts.

The literature reviewed in this chapter represents theories and their applications to tenancy pertinent to my study of the causes of the decline in tenant contracts relative to wage contracts. The theoretical work on transactions costs and risk-bearing provides me with a framework on which to build my model: transactions costs and risk-bearing vary among contracts. To explain the mix of contracts across time and between regions, it is necessary to specify measureable variables which influence either risk or transactions costs. The empirical work reviewed, along with USDA bulletins, indicate possible causes of the demise of tenancy: mechanization, changes in crop mix or labor scarcity, urbanization and increased crop yields. In Chapter 2, the relationship between these variables in a theory of risk and transactions costs will be formally specified and modeled.

Chapter 2

A Theory of the Decline in Tenant Contracts Relative to Wage Contracts in the South, 1930-1960

Agricultural labor contracts during the period 1930-1960 most frequently took the form of a fixed cash wage per specified time period, a fixed cash rental or an output share rental. The existence of the observed mix of contracts can be explained by the varying risk dispersal and transactions costs attributes of the different labor contracts. To explain changes in contractual choice over time and differences in contractual choice across regions, it is necessary to dichotomize the continuum of contracts because, for any given change in transactions costs, the effect on the resulting number of share contracts is ambiguous. Suppose that, as transactions costs fall, fixed rent and share contracting are no longer as desirable relative to wage contracts. We can unambiguously predict that the number of fixed rentals will fall as the parties shift into either share or fixed wage contracts. Fixed wage contracts will unambiguously rise as former fixed rent and share contractors change to fixed wage. The net effect on the number of share contracts is ambiguous because some share rent contractors will shift into fixed wage contracts, causing a decline in the number of share contracts, but simultaneously the number of share contracts will be increased by some fixed renters shifting into share contracts. Depending on the magnitudes of these two effects, share contracts could either increase or decrease. The impact of a fall in transactions costs can be illustrated by means of the following diagram.

Whenever transactions costs or risk change, the net effect on share contracts is indeterminate due to incentives to shift both into and out of share contracts. For this reason, the variable I will explain is the number of tenant contracts (the summation of share tenants and fixed-rent tenants) relative to the number of fixed wage contracts.

Ideally, we would like to derive generalized transactions cost and risk functions to aid in predicting the relative changes in tenant contracts. Unfortunately, the present theoretical and empirical work on contracting is limited to specifying causal factors which affect either transactions costs or risk. In this chapter I will discuss how risk and transactions costs vary between contractual forms. In addition, I will develop testable hypotheses concerning contractual choices after examining those causal factors influencing risk and transactions costs. The research presented is best viewed as a contribution to the development of a more general theory of the costs of contracting.

Transactions costs associated with agricultural contracts include negotiation, supervision and enforcement costs. Negotiation costs are the costs incurred in reaching the terms of the contract and are borne by both the employer and employee. Supervision costs result from efforts expended to obtain the amount of labor input stipulated by the contract. Enforcement costs refer to the expense involved in ensuring that labor will honor the length of the contract. In order to explain changes in contractual choice, it is necessary to specify how transactions costs vary under different contractual forms as well as to identify who bears the costs. Negotiations costs appear to be invariant with respect to contractual form. In a market with many similar competing parties, the terms of the contract are given to both contractors. Considering the number of landlords and tenants in agriculture, the assumption of such "price-taking competition" is reasonable. Even if monopolistic or monopsonistic influences raise the total costs of negotiating a contract, differences in negotiation costs between different forms of contracts would remain zero.

Supervision costs are borne entirely by the landowner and vary among contracts. Supervision costs are the largest under wage contracts and the smallest under fixed rent contracts. Because fixed wage payments are not a function of total output, workers have an incentive to shirk. Because the payment to labor under a share contract is a function of output, the worker has an incentive to increase output and, as a result, costs are less than under a wage contract. Nevertheless, unless supervised, the laborer will not work up to the optimal point from the landlord's point of view. A worker stops supplying labor services when his share of the additional output just equals his opportunity cost. The smaller the share of the output that labor is to receive, the greater the supervision costs required. Under the limiting case of a fixed cash rental contract negotiated in perpetuity, supervision costs are zero. Since the payment to the landlord is not a function of output, the landlord could not increase his income by supervising the tenant. If the cash rent contract covers a finite period of time, then some supervision costs are necessary to insure that the tenant maximizes the return on the asset (land) from the landlord's point of view. Specifications of the type of crop and farming practices are examples of the supervision that would be required.

Enforcement costs also vary across contractual forms and, like supervision costs, are borne entirely by the landowner. The larger the difference between the expected income from honoring a contract's length and the opportunity cost to labor of alternative employment, the smaller are the enforcement costs. Expected income for labor is greater under tenant contracts than under wage contracts, because labor receives a risk premium and requires less supervision. Specifying the factors that affect supervision and enforcement costs will enable us to predict the direction of change of contractual choice. When either supervision or enforcement costs increase, we should observe a relative shift into tenant contracts as a result of efforts by the landowners to reduce costs. The landowner is now willing to pay a larger premium to induce labor to absorb some of the increase in transactions costs.

Risk-averse individuals seek to avoid risk if the costs of doing so are less than the gains from the averted risk. If there exists among individuals a probability distribution of preferences towards risk, then we should observe the use of all three types of contracts, because varying amounts or distributions of risk are associated with each contract.

The income risk associated with agricultural production

is composed of price risk and output risk. Under a fixed cash rental, the tenant bears all of the risk associated with fluctuations in prices and output, whereas under a fixed wage contract, all of the risk is borne by the employer. Share contracts spread both output and price risk between tenant and landlord. Since the mid-1930's, price risk has been substantially reduced, regardless of contractual form, by federal price supports. Output risk, which is largely a function of the vagaries of weather, has remained. For this reason, I will use output risk as a proxy for income risk.

Agriculture in the Southern cotton states was predominantly composed of farms growing only one cash crop, cotton. The output risk associated with cotton farming is approximated by the variability of cotton yields. I will assume, as did Higgs, that the total amount of risk borne by the two parties is identical under all three contracts.[1] Only the proportion of the total borne by each party differs. It is reasonable to assume that, as a class, agricultural workers are relatively more risk averse than landowners because they are less wealthy and have less

---

[1] Robert Higgs, "Race, Tenure and Resource Allocation in Southern Agriculture, 1910," *Journal of Economic History*, XXXIII (March 1973).

access to credit markets. If agricultural workers are willing to pay a higher price than landowners to avoid risk (by shifting it onto the landlord), we would expect a fall in the contractual form which minimizes the amount of risk borne by the workers, when the absolute amount of risk is reduced. I will specify below factors that have reduced the risk of cotton farming in the South.

The relative number of tenant contracts is determined by both the demand for agricultural contracts by landowners and the supply of agricultural contracts by labor.[2] The expected compensation for labor services under a tenant contract exceeds the fixed (definite) payment to labor under a wage contract. The smaller the difference between these two payments, the more desirable a tenant contract becomes in the eyes of the landowner, because of the smaller premiums paid to labor as compensation for bearing more risk and requiring less supervision. Labor, on the other hand, is willing to supply fewer tenant contracts as the difference between the expected tenant compensation and fixed wage narrows. These hypotheses are subject to the conditions that there exist given levels of risk and transactions costs. The landowners' demand (eq. #1) and workers' supply

---

The following is an extension of a model developed by Robert Higgs in "Race, Tenure and Resource Allocation in Southern Agriculture, 1910." My contribution is an explicit analysis of transactions costs.

(eq. #2) of tenant relative to wage contracts can be expressed in the following functional notation:

$$(1) \qquad T/W = \alpha_0 + \alpha_1 D + \alpha_2 \sigma + \alpha_3 S + \alpha_4 E$$

$$(2) \qquad T/W = \beta_0 + \beta_1 D + \beta_2 \sigma$$

where T/W = (tenant contracts)/(wage contracts),

D = difference between expected labor compensation under tenant and wage contracts

σ = risk level

S = supervision costs

E = enforcement costs

In the landowners' demand equation: $\alpha_1 < 0$ (as the difference becomes larger, landowners will increasingly prefer to bear the risk and transactions costs themselves rather than pay for it in the market); $\alpha_2 > 0$ (assuming risk aversion); $\alpha_3 > 0$ (as the costs of supervising labor rise, landlords are less willing to supervise labor); $\alpha_4 > 0$ (as enforcement costs rise, landowners are less willing to enforce compliance with the length of the contract). In the workers' supply equation: $\beta_1 > 0$ (as the premium paid for risk-bearing supervision and enforcement increases, workers will desire more of the contracts under which they receive this premium); $\beta_2 < 0$ (assuming risk aversion).

The equilibrium mix of contracts is determined by the interaction of supply and demand for contracts. The reduced form solution for the dependent variable, (T/W), is:

$$(3)\ T/W = \frac{(\alpha_1\beta_2 - \beta_1\alpha_2)\sigma - \beta_1\alpha_3 S - \beta_1\alpha_4 E + (\alpha_1\beta_0 - \alpha_0\beta_1)}{\alpha_1 - \beta_1}$$

Assuming relative risk aversion, the coefficient for the risk variable is negative. Workers are willing to pay a relatively greater price than landlords require to retain the prior contractual mix when the level of risk increases. In theory, the coefficients for supervision costs and enforcements costs should be positive. A change in risk is depicted in Figure 1. If the level of risk increases, the supply curve will pivot back more than the demand curve pivots out. At the new equilibrium, the relative number of tenant to wage contracts will be smaller: T/W_2.

The effect of a change in supervision costs and enforcements costs is shown in Figure 2. An increase in either supervision or enforcement costs will pivot the demand for tenant contracts by landowners out and relatively more tenant contracts will be adopted. The landlord is now willing to pay a greater premium (D) to workers in an effort to reduce transactions costs.

Before estimating the reduced form equation 3, I will

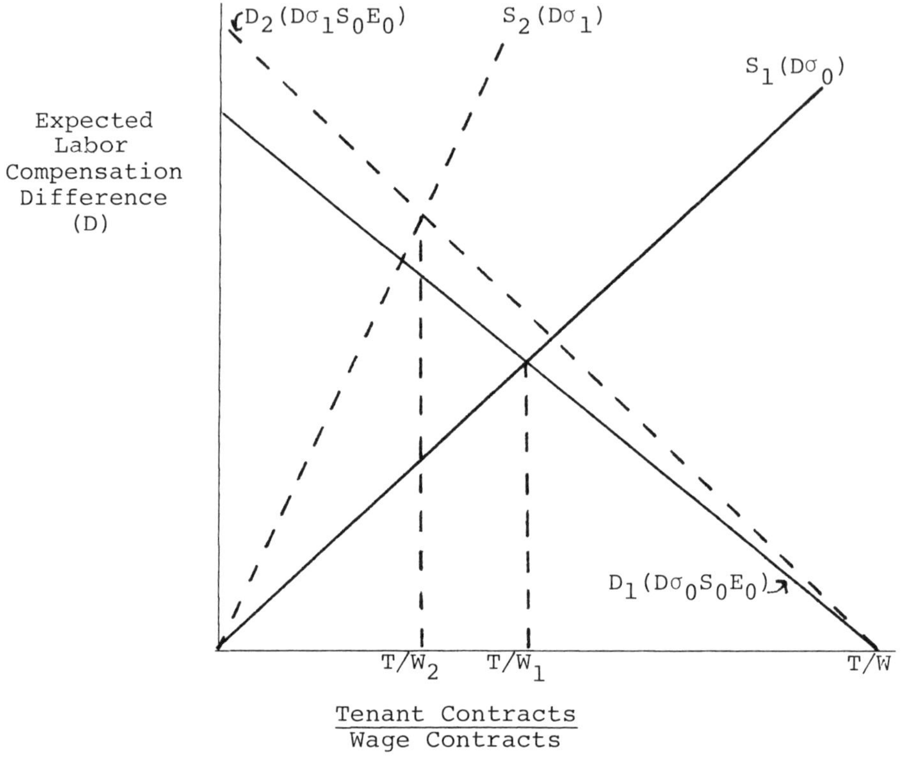

Figure 1. Equilibrium Mix of Contracts--Risk Changing

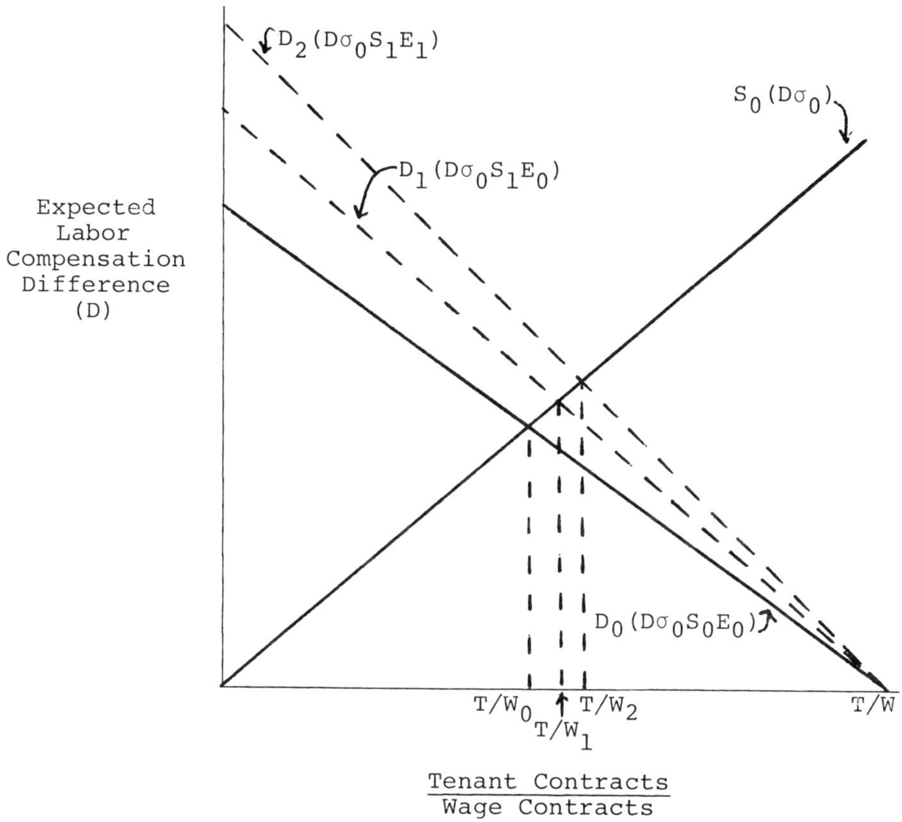

Figure 2. Equilibrium Mix of Contracts--Transactions Costs Changing

specify in detail the variables that have affected either risk or transactions costs.

Several factors have contributed to the different contractual mix observed in each of the ten states at any given point in time and to the change in mix over time. The factors that I believe significantly affected either transactions costs or risk include the number of tractors relative to the number of horses and mules, the unemployment rate, the degree of urbanization, crop yields and crop mix. Each of these influences will be presented as a testable hypothesis.

When the number of tractors relative to the number of horses and mules rises, we should observe a fall in the relative number of tenants. Although it has been recognized in numerous agricultural bulletins that wage labor is associated with farms that employ tractors,[3] no theory has been

---

Arkansas Agricultural Experiment Station, "Changes in Labor Organization on Cotton Farms," by J.G. McNeely and Glen T. Barton, Bulletin No. 397 (Fayetteville, Arkansas: June 1940), p. 19; United States Department of Agriculture, "Plantation Organization and Operation in the Yazoo-Mississippi Delta Area," by E.L. Langsford and B.N. Thibodeaux, Technical Bulletin No. 682 (Washington, D.C.: Government Printing Office, May 1939), pp. 27, 52; Arkansas Agricultural Experiment Station, "Further Changes in Labor Used on Cotton Farms, 1939-1944," by Otis J. Osgood and John W. White, Bulletin No. 459 (Fayetteville, Arkansas: August 1945), p. 23; Mississippi State College Agricultural Experiment Station, "Farm Mechanization in the Upland Areas of Mississippi, 1949," by Rupert B. Johnson, Bulletin No. 520 (State College, Mississippi: July 1953), p. 6.

presented to explain this correlation. Tractors, as compared with the alternative power source (horses and mules), reduce both total labor supervision costs (through the displacement of labor) and supervision costs per unit of labor. Because it lacks discretion, a machine's performance is comparatively uniform. The difficulty of duplicating the dexterity of the human hand long retarded the mechanization of cotton cultivation. But once tractor power was adopted, along with various other implements, standardization of production was introduced.[4] Whether the quality of work obtained by employing the tractor technique was reduced or raised is not the issue. What is crucial is that it became easier to measure labor input when employing the tractor, since the variance of the quality of labor's output (e.g., quality of rows plowed) is smaller. By assessing the acreage plowed or measuring the quantity of gasoline consumed by the tractor, a landowner could monitor a combination of tractor and labor inputs more cheaply than he could a combination of animal and labor inputs.

As the relative supply of labor falls, we expect the relative number of tenants to rise. When employment rates rise, alternative employment opportunities increase and this

---

[4] James H. Street, _The New Revolution in the Cotton Economy_ (Chapel Hill: University of North Carolina Press, 1957), pp. 100, 235.

in turn raises enforcement costs since labor's incentive to renege on a contract is greater.[5] Numerous studies have identified the correspondence between tenant contracts and labor scarcity[6] but no theoretical rationale has been provided. An additional impetus for wage contracts to increase as unemployment rose was that tenants were classified as farm operators and were therefore ineligible for all or a portion of federal government unemployment benefits.[7]

As the degree of urbanization increases, we expect a decline in the relative number of tenants. If labor does not fulfill the length of the contract, an employer situated near an urban area has a larger total population to draw from for replacements. To this extent, the costs of losing labor during the year fall, which in turn will reduce the attraction of tenant contracts.

---

[5] In Chapter 1 I discuss in detail the reason why tenant contracts secure labor better than wage contracts.

[6] Street, *op. cit.*, pp. 218, 228; United States Department of Agriculture, "Relation of Land Tenure to Plantation Organization," Bulletin No. 1269 (Washington, D.C.: Government Printing Office, 1924), pp. 22, 38; Arkansas Agricultural Experiment Station, "Further Changes in Labor Used on Cotton Farms, 1939-1944," p. 29; United States Department of Agriculture, "Plantation Organization and Operation in the Yazoo-Mississippi Delta Area," p. 87.

[7] Arkansas Agricultural Experiment Station, "The Farm Tenancy Situation," by J.A. Baker and J.G. McNeely, Bulletin No. 384 (Fayetteville, Arkansas: January 1940), p. 30.

H.W. Blalock, in a survey of 89 plantations in Arkansas, noted increased usage of wage labor on plantations located near centers of population such as Memphis, Little Rock, Pine Bluff and Texarkana. Blalock found that "plantations located near centers of population had an average wage crop of 353 acres and paid 31.4 percent of their wages to labor living away from the plantations; plantations removed from centers of population had an average wage crop of only 179 acres and paid 20.8 percent in wages to laborers living away from the plantations."[8] The percentage of wages paid to regular wage hands living on the farm was 42.3 percent for plantations located near urban areas, as compared to 34.3 percent for rural plantations.[9] Blalock's explanation of this difference was that the available supply of wage labor was greater the closer it was to an urban area. While his argument is not rigorous, his findings are consistent with my hypothesis.

As the risk in cotton farming rises, we expect the relative number of tenants to fall; tenants are willing to pay a larger premium than landlords to avoid the increased risk. Output risk can be represented by the coefficient of

---

[8] Arkansas Agricultural Experiment Station, "Plantation Operations of Landlords and Tenants in Arkansas," by H.W. Blalock, Bulletin No. 339 (Fayetteville, Arkansas: May 1937), p. 13.

[9] *Ibid.*, p. 43.

variation of cotton yields, but data on this variable are not available. I will use cotton yields as an indicator of risk in farming because, in all the states considered, cotton was the main cash crop grown, and evidence from agricultural bulletins strongly indicates that as average yields rise, the variance of yields declines. John L. Fulmer and Ralph R. Botts, in a survey of 707 cotton belt counties from 1938 to 1946, found that an increase in county average yield was the most significant factor in accounting for reduction in variation.[10] Given relative risk aversion by tenants, a decrease in risk will reduce the relative frequency of fixed wage contracts.

As the percentage of total acreage in cotton rises, the number of tenants relative to wage workers should rise.[11] The production of cotton, as compared to the production of feed crops or other soil conserving crops (e.g., legumes, hay) requires more intensive cultivation. Numerous studies indicate that the labor requirements for cotton are at least twice as great as for either corn, soybeans or hay,

---

[10] United States Department of Agriculture, "Analysis of Factors Influencing Cotton Yields and Their Variability," by John L. Fulmer and Ralph R. Botts, Technical Bulletin No. 1042 (Washington, D.C.: Government Printing Office, October 1951), p. 26.

[11] I am assuming that, given price expectations of crop inputs and crop outputs, farmers first decide on the wealth maximizing crop mix and then negotiate the least costly labor contractual arrangement.

even when a tractor is employed.[12] Rising labor requirements increase total supervision costs. In an effort to reduce supervision costs, contractors will enter into more tenant contracts when cotton acreage increases.

Many contemporary sources have pointed out the association between cotton and tenancy.[13] The rationale generally given for utilizing tenant labor on cotton acreage is that it required extensive hand labor.[14] The implication is that it was costly to monitor hand labor, and incentives for labor to supervise its own work could be provided by tenant contracts. Not only are total and relative labor supervision costs greater for cotton than for other potential crops, but there is also a peak labor demand problem[15]

---

[12] United States Department of Agriculture, "Plantation Organization and Operation in the Yazoo-Mississippi Delta Area," pp. 58, 60, 64-65, 67; John L. Fulmer, Agricultural Progress in the Cotton Belt Since 1920 (Chapel Hill: University of North Carolina Press, 1950), p. 61; U.S. Works Progress Administration and USDA Bureau of Agricultural Economics Co-operating, Studies of Changing Techniques and Employment in Agriculture, Report No. 15 (Washington, D.C.: Government Printing Office, 1941), pp. 114-150.

[13] Arkansas Agricultural Experiment Station, "Further Changes in Labor Used on Cotton Farms," p. 15; U.S. Department of Agriculture, "Relation of Land Tenure to Plantation Organization," p. 55; U.S. Department of Agriculture, "Plantation Organization and Operation in the Yazoo-Mississippi Delta Area," pp. 22, 41, 59-60.

[14] U.S. Department of Agriculture, "Plantation Organization and Operation in the Yazoo-Mississippi Delta Area," p. 22.

[15] Arkansas Agricultural Experiment Station, "Changes in

associated with cotton. Due to increases in demand at harvest time, enforcing a contract becomes more costly because alternative employment opportunities for labor increase (cotton picking elsewhere at piece rates). The combined effects of increasing supervision and enforcement costs reinforce a shift into tenant contracts.

Alternatively, if the percentage of either legumes or corn rises, the relative number of wage contracts should increase. Wage labor was typically employed in the production of noncash crops (e.g., corn, legumes).[16] Labor requirements are reduced when corn or legumes are planted instead of cotton, and consequently supervision costs fall. Enforcement costs will also fall because neither corn nor legumes present a peak labor demand problem.

---

[16] Arkansas Agricultural Experiment Station, "Plantation Operations of Landlords and Tenants in Arkansas," pp. 6, 9-10; U.S. Works Progress Administration and USDA Bureau of Agricultural Economics Co-operating, pp. 106-107; U.S. Department of Agriculture, "Relation of Land Tenure to Plantation Organization," p. 60.

Labor Organization on Cotton Farms," pp. 16-17; U.S. Department of Agriculture, "Plantation Organization and Operation in the Yazoo-Mississippi Delta Area," p. 59.

Chapter 3

Empirical Results

In this chapter I will specify and test econometrically my model and present the empirical results. The regression analysis is not designed to test competing hypotheses developed by other scholars. Their hypotheses assume that the terms of tenant contracts were inflexible but because evidence indicates that adjustments in contracts took place, their hypotheses cannot be logically derived from their models.

I will test the hypotheses that I developed in Chapter 2 using county data from ten Southern states for the period 1930-1960. The states considered are North Carolina, South Carolina, Georgia, Tennessee, Alabama, Mississippi, Arkansas, Louisiana, Oklahoma and Texas. I collected data on 25 sample counties from each state for each of the census years 1930, 1940, 1945, 1950, 1954 and 1959.[1]

The dependent variable in all of the regressions is the number of tenants divided by total real dollars paid for farm wage labor. Dollars paid for farm labor is a better proxy for wage contracts than the number of persons hired, because persons hired gives us very little indication of

---

[1] See Appendix A for the location of the sample counties.

the amount of labor services provided. (Whether someone was hired for one hour a week or 60 hours a week, one person was recorded as hired; yet totally different conditions are implied by the two cases.)

The explanatory variables included in the regression analysis are as follows:

Tr = Tractors/(Horses + Mules)

Co = Cotton Acreage Harvested/Total Cropland Harvested

Cn = Corn Acreage Harvested/Total Cropland Harvested

Le = Legume Acreage Harvested/Total Cropland Harvested

U = Urban Population/Total Population

E = Persons Employed/Labor Force

Y = Bales of Cotton/Cotton Acreage Harvested

$D1_t$ = Dummy Variable for Time, 5 = 1930, 1940, 1945, 1950, 1954, 1959

$D2_i$ = Dummy Variable for States, i = NC, ..., TX

Except for the degree of urbanization and the percentage of the labor force employed, observations for all the variables are available for all six census periods. The regression equations which include urbanization and employment variables are estimated with only 1000 of the 1500 observations (i.e., data for 1945 and 1954 are omitted). The specification for all of the equations is log linear. The regression results are presented in Table 2.

In the first equation all of the coefficients are

Table 2

Estimated Regression Coefficients;

Dependent Variable (Tenants/Wages)

Explanatory Variables	Equation 1	2	3	4	5
Constant	-8.29	-8.31	-8.50	-8.38	-9.82
Tractors/ (Horses + Mules)	-0.82 (-45.92)*	-0.90 (-37.52)*	-0.41 (-14.51)*	-0.36 (-10.44)*	-0.39 (-11.80)*
Cotton Acres	0.03 (4.08)*	0.04 (3.47)*	0.04 (6.09)*	0.04 (5.43)*	0.04 (5.06)*
Corn Acres	0.22 (9.43)*	0.18 (6.00)*	0.30 (15.03)*	0.29 (11.73)*	0.11 (3.65)*
Legume Acres	-0.11 (-6.24)*	-0.09 (-3.97)*	-0.15 (-9.50)*	-0.14 (-7.35)*	-0.13 (-7.40)*
Cotton Yields	-0.25 (-3.89)*	-0.10 (-1.05)	-0.09 (-1.48)*	0.04 (0.50)	-0.10 (-1.21)
Percent Urban		-0.02 (-1.90)*		-0.02 (-1.55)**	-0.02 (-1.59)**
Employment Rate		0.05 (0.14)		0.96 (3.65)*	0.19 (0.69)
Time Dummy Variables for:					
1930			2.18 (14.87)*	2.54 (13.66)*	2.46 (14.05)*
1940			2.78 (22.09)*	3.00 (20.78)*	3.02 (22.27)*
1945			1.27 (11.84)*		
1950			0.78 (8.27)*	0.89 (8.79)*	0.86 (9.20)*

Table 2. Estimated Regression Coefficients (continued)

Explanatory Variables	Equation 1	2	3	4	5
Time Dummy Variables for (continued):					
1955			0.74 (8.75)*		
State Dummy Variables for (excluded state: Texas):					
NC					1.18 (8.00)*
SC					0.98 (7.12)*
GA					1.18 (8.46)*
TE					1.26 (8.32)*
AL					1.51 (10.29)*
MI					1.66 (11.16)*
AR					1.03 (7.77)*
LO					0.33 (2.56)*
OK					1.16 (9.59)*

Table 2. Estimated Regression Coefficients (continued)

Explanatory Variable	Equation 1	2	3	4	5
$\bar{R}^2$	0.71	0.74	0.79	0.82	0.85

* Significant at the 95% confidence level.
** Significant at the 90% confidence level.

t values in parentheses.

statistically significant at the 0.99 confidence level. The signs of the coefficients for tractors, cotton acreage and legume acreage are consistent with my theory, whereas the coefficients obtained for corn acreage and cotton yields are inconsistent with my hypotheses. Adding urbanization and employment to the equation does not affect most of the coefficients. However, in equation 1, yields are apparently capturing some of the influence of employment and urbanization, because with the addition of these variables, the coefficient on cotton yields becomes insignificant. It is plausible that cotton yields are not a satisfactory proxy for risk. The insignificance of the employment coefficient may be due to structural differences in labor markets in different time periods. Social legislation, such as minimum wage laws and welfare programs, produced a continual rise in the equilibrium rate of unemployment. Unless the observations are adjusted to reflect this rise, the explanatory power of the labor scarcity variable will be obscured. For example, a 4 percent unemployment rate in 1940 could have been "high" while the same rate in 1960 could have been associated with a tight labor market. Dummy variables for time are added in equation 3 in an effort to control for the downward trend in the employment rate and for other time trends not captured by the specification in equation 3.

Equation 3 is estimated using the entire data set. The

coefficients on the dummy variables for time are relative to the excluded period, 1960, and are all significant at the 99 percent confidence level. The coefficients increase in size from 1930 to 1940 and then taper off, indicating that the inherent structural influences mentioned above grew progressively closer to their 1960 condition during the period 1940-1960.

In equation 4, where employment and urbanization variables are included in the regression equation along with the dummy variables for time, observations from 1945 and 1955 must be deleted. The coefficients on the included dummy variables remain relatively constant. As expected, the coefficient of the employment variable becomes highly significant when a control is made for the influence of time. The coefficients on crop mix are unchanged and, as in equation 2, the influence of cotton yields on tenancy is not statistically different from zero.

In equation 5, dummy variables for each of the states are added to control for the influence of location. The coefficients on tractors, cotton, legumes, urbanization and time remain constant and significant. The total explanatory power of the equation increases slightly and the influence of employment and corn decreases. The information provided by the employment variable in equation 4 is now conveyed by state location, implying that state location may be a better proxy for labor scarcity than employment rates. Controlling for state location also reduces the coefficient on corn, indicating that the same percentage of total acreage in corn in each state implies different levels of tenancy. It is therefore plausible that the marginal influence of corn acreage also varies among states.

In order to test the null hypotheses that the differences between the coefficients on the state dummy variables, in any combination of two states, is equal to zero, I ran equation 5 excluding a different state dummy variable each time. The differences in the coefficients on the dummy variable for states, relative to the coefficient on the dummy variable for the excluded state, are reported in Table 3. The appropriate method to make multiple comparisons of parameters is the S-test.[2] Both Louisiana and Texas display significantly lower levels of tenancy than all other states, _ceteris paribus_.[3]

---

[2] Henry Scheffé, _The Analysis of Variance_ (New York: John Wiley & Sons, Inc., 1959), p. 66.

[3] If there are large differences in wage rates among counties or states, dollars paid for wage labor (denominator of the dependent variable) is an inadequate proxy for the number of wage contracts. An examination of the data on wage rates indicates that they do not significantly vary among states and therefore cannot account for differences in the T/W ratio among states. For data on average wage rates in the ten states studied, consult: U.S. Department of Agriculture, _Statistics on Cotton and Related Data, 1930-1967_, Statistical Bulletin No. 417 (Washington, D.C.: Government Printing Office, 1968), p. 99.

Table 3

Regression Coefficients for State Dummy Variables

(Table 2, Equation 5 Specification)†

Excluded State	Constant	LO	SC	AR	OK	GA	NC	TE	AL	MI
TX	-9.82	0.33	0.98	1.03	1.16	1.18	1.18	1.26	1.51	1.66
	(0.16)	(0.13)	(0.14)*	(0.13)*	(0.12)*	(0.14)*	(0.15)*	(0.15)*	(0.15)*	(0.15)*
LO	-9.48		0.65	0.69	0.83	0.84	0.85	0.93	1.18	1.32
	(0.13)		(0.12)*	(0.12)*	(0.13)*	(0.12)*	(0.13)*	(0.13)*	(0.13)*	(0.13)*
SC	-8.84			0.04	0.18	0.20	0.20	0.28	0.53	0.68
	(0.12)			(0.12)	(0.13)	(0.12)	(0.13)	(0.13)	(0.13)**	(0.12)*
AR	-8.79				0.13	0.15	0.15	0.23	0.49	0.63
	(0.13)				(0.13)	(0.12)	(0.13)	(0.13)	(0.13)	(0.12)*
OK	-8.65					0.02	0.02	0.10	0.35	0.50
	(0.16)					(0.13)	(0.13)	(0.14)	(0.14)	(0.14)
GA	-8.64						0.002	0.08	0.33	0.48
	(0.12)						(0.13)	(0.12)	(0.14)	(0.13)
NC	-8.64							0.08	0.34	0.48
	(0.13)							(0.13)	(0.13)	(0.12)**
TE	-8.56								0.26	0.40
	(0.13)								(0.14)	(0.13)

Table 3. Regression Coefficients for State Dummy Variables (continued)

Excluded State	Constant	LO	SC	AR	OK	GA	NC	TE	AL	MI
AL	-8.30 (0.12)									0.14 (0.13)
MI	-8.16 (0.11)									

† Coefficients on the other explanatory variables are presented in Table 2, Equation 5.
* Significant at 95% confidence level (S-test)
** Significant at 90% confidence level (S-test)

Standard error given in parentheses.

The availability of Mexican wage labor and prevalence of sugar cultivation are two factors that might account for the relative predominance of wage contracts in Texas and Louisiana. The availability of Mexican labor at harvest time eliminates the necessity to negotiate a tenant contract in order to secure a labor force. Sugar cultivation, which is more common in Louisiana than elsewhere in the South, requires extensive coordination of the stages of production and close supervision and therefore has historically utilized wage labor.

Because the addition of state location to regression equation 5 affected the explanatory power of the variables, corn and employment, it is reasonable to suspect that the marginal relationship between the dependent variable and the explanatory variables corn and employment varies among states. In order to test whether there exist differences among the ten states in the marginal relationship between tenancy and the two explanatory variables, corn acreage and the employment rate, I have estimated equation 5 twice; once with the addition of separate state categories for the variable corn acreage and again with separate state categories for the employment rate variable. The total explanatory power of the equation is not changed substantially, nor are the coefficients on the remaining explanatory variables altered. The coefficients of the explanatory variables corn acreage and employment rate, separated in state categories, are presented in Table 4. Of the six employment coefficients that are significant, five are consistent with my hypothesis. Five of the six significant coefficients on corn acreage are inconsistent with the theory presented in this chapter. No explanation for the sign on the employment coefficient for Alabama is apparent. The sign on the corn acreage variable could be due to aggregation bias inherent in my random sampling technique. If corn is not as likely to be grown in every county of the state, bias in my estimates may result. For example, in the western region of Texas, very little corn is grown. The land is utilized primarily for cattle grazing or for irrigated cotton and wheat. Cash wages have customarily been paid to labor in this area. Therefore, corn acreage in eastern Texas appears to be associated with tenancy because there exists very little tenancy or corn acreage in the western part of the state. Given the amount of contemporary evidence indicating that corn acreage is associated with wage labor, it is probable that the observed correlation in my regression results is not causal but spurious. In order to test this assertion, it would be necessary to construct a stratified sample excluding counties which have less than a certain percentage of total acreage in corn.

Table 4

Regression Coefficients of the Employment Rate and Corn Acreage Variables for State Categories (Table 2, Equation 5 Specification)†

State	Employment Rate Times Dummy Variable for State	Corn Acreage Times Dummy Variable for State
NC	5.89 (3.52)*	0.38 (1.36)**
SC	10.02 (3.87)*	-0.33 (-1.39)**
GA	11.23 (3.32)*	0.24 (0.94)
TE	2.15 (1.60)**	1.05 (4.55)*
AL	-0.70 (-1.86)*	0.32 (0.76)
MI	0.99 (1.15)	(0.17) (2.91)*
AR	0.99 (0.72)	0.12 (0.87)
LO	4.45 (3.18)*	0.24 (3.10)*
OK	0.20 (0.27)	-0.06 (-1.15)
TX	-0.73 (-0.41)	0.14 (3.34)*
$\bar{R}^2$	0.8598	0.8598
F-statistic	3.99*	4.01*

Table 4. Regression Coefficients for Employment Rate and Corn Acreage Variables for State Categories (continued)

† Coefficients on the other explanatory variables did not change and are presented in Table 2, equation 5.
* Significant at 99% confidence level.
** Significant at 90% confidence level.

t values in parentheses.

In summary, the aim of this research is to explain the relative decline in agricultural tenant contracts in the South from 1930 to 1960. A theory has been developed based on differences in transactions costs and risk among labor contracts. In general, the empirical results are consistent with the hypotheses implied by the theory. Mechanization dramatically reduced supervision costs and was the most influential factor in accounting for the relative decline of tenancy. Cotton cultivation requires relatively more supervision than other crops and, as expected, increases in cotton acreage were associated with more tenancy. Legume cultivation, on the other hand, by reducing supervision costs, significantly increased the desirability of wage contracts. The finding that increases in corn acreage raise the relative number of tenant contracts is at odds with the hypothesis developed in Chapter 2 and may be due to aggregation bias inherent in my sample. The regression results are consistent with the hypothesis that urbanization, by reducing search costs, increases the prevalence of wage contracts. The employment rate variable is not statistically significant, which may be due to structural differences in labor markets between the states not captured by the data. Risk does not possess much explanatory power in my results. Perhaps it was not important during this time period; or perhaps cotton yields are not an adequate proxy for risk. In general, given the empirical results obtained, the general hypothesis that a decline in transactions costs resulted in relatively fewer tenant contracts is strongly supported.

Chapter 4

Wage Contracting and Race Relations in the Plantation South

The causal factors underlying the shift from tenant contracts to wage contracts have been analyzed in earlier chapters. This change in the predominant contractual form was accompanied by considerable changes in the components of labor compensation under both tenant and wage contracts. Most notable was the substitution of cash payments for fringe benefits. The purpose of this chapter is to investigate the impact of the relative rise in wage contracts and the increased use of cash payments on race relations, which also underwent a substantial transformation during the period under consideration. The following hypotheses are primarily applicable to race relations in the rural plantation South. The rural plantation South includes principally large farms, many of which had been slave plantations, employing numerous tenants. Rural counties in South Carolina, Georgia, Alabama, Mississippi, Louisiana and Arkansas in which over half the population was black fit this classification.

In general, labor contracts stipulate benefits other than a specified number of dollars for labor services. These other benefits are typically referred to as fringe benefits. In the South around 1930, most agricultural labor contracts contained many fringe benefits, including items which were subject to negotiation, such as a house, garden plots, grazing rights for cattle, firewood, wagon and mule use, hunting privileges and the amount of credit at the plantation store.[1] In addition, some benefits received were implicit and not subject to negotiation. These included such diverse items as contributions to the black church and school, a white protector who saw that justice was served (provided that the issues did not entail infractions against the prevailing race relations), income supplements after retirement, and funeral services.[2] H.W. Blalock, in a study of 89 plantations in Arkansas in 1934, found that landlords often assisted tenants in payment of medical expenses and court fines, and provided general entertainment for the tenants and their children.[3] It must

---

[1] See, for example: Arthur R. Raper, Preface to Peasantry (New York: Atheneum, 1974), p. 52; Hortense Powdermaker, After Freedom (New York: Atheneum, 1968), p. 82; Charles S. Johnson, Shadow of the Plantation (Chicago: University of Chicago Press, 1966), p. 115; William Alexander Percy, Lanterns on the Levee (New York: Alfred A. Knopf, 1941), p. 276.

[2] See, for example: Morton Rubin, Plantation County (Chapel Hill: University of North Carolina Press, 1951), pp. 32, 100; U.S. Department of Agriculture, "Relation of Land Tenure to Plantation Organization," by C.O. Brannen, Bulletin No. 1269 (Washington, D.C.: Government Printing Office, 1924), p. 49; Raper, *op. cit.*, pp. 84, 157, 293, 360; Johnson, *op. cit.*, p. 191.

[3] Arkansas Agricultural Experiment Station, "Plantation

be remembered that there was no standardized list of benefits and that the variance from landlord to landlord was immense.

In return for these fringes, blacks were expected to show respect and to know their "place," which in general meant playing a subservient role to whites:

> Sam Eades is a "good Negro." He behaves strictly in accordance with the race-caste code when dealing with white people. He "gets along"; he isn't looking for trouble; he is humble above all. He is a "good Negro" if he smiles and appears happy. By inclining his head, Sam shows the white man that he acknowledges him as superior. He tips his hat to white men and women. He does not look a white woman straight in the eye. Sam treats all whites, from the "sorriest" poor white to the wealthiest "high type" white from the plantation with the same deference. He waits until a white person is disengaged before approaching for conversation, even though his own business may be of more importance to each than some trivia that might be under discussion. He says "sir" or "ma'am" at all times, punctuating his conversation frequently with these titles of courtesy.[4]

Landlords functioned as intermediaries between tenants and the outside world. Security and isolation were the norms for many tenant families. In times of illness in

---

[4] Rubin, op. cit., p. 90.

Operations of Landlords and Tenants in Arkansas," by H.W. Blalock, Bulletin No. 339 (Fayetteville, Arkansas: May 1937), p. 37.

tenant families, the landlord frequently decided if a doctor should be called. Tenants sought advice on marriages, divorces and burials. Tenant children were told when and how long to attend school. Taxes were paid and cotton was sold by the landlord. Blacks on plantations had few dealings in the market. Necessities were purchased on credit at the plantation store and the money left over after settlement (if any) was generally funnelled back to the commissary. A tenant's life centered around his farm and his church.[5]

I am not maintaining that because an exchange of sorts was taking place, blacks had a choice about the role they assumed in the labor exchange but, rather, that, given the existing socioeconomic institutional framework in existence around 1930, blacks had economic incentives to adopt a subservient role. The close association between work and social life promoted both economic and social dependence.

As agricultural labor contracts in the rural South began to incorporate fewer in-kind and social benefits, the overall dependence of blacks on whites declined. _The use of cash increased partly because of the shift from tenant to wage contracts_. Cash was generally the method of payment

---

[5] Rubin, _ibid_., pp. 66-67; Johnson, _op. cit_., p. 27; Rosengarten, _All God's Dangers_ (New York: Avon, 1975), pp. 125, 185, 202-203, 212.

with wage contracts because it offered advantages to both the wage workers and the landlord. A wage worker, because he was less permanent than a tenant, was less willing to wait until harvest time to be paid, and consequently he received pay more frequently. Given frequent pay periods, the costs of converting income in kind (cotton) into consumption becomes exceedingly costly because of frequent trips to the cotton gin. For the landlord, cash was easier to store or borrow than in-kind payments. In addition, both landlord and worker gain by having a non-perishable form of payment.

Wage contracts also embodied fewer fringe benefits than tenant contracts. Because wage workers are more transient, certain indivisible fringe benefits such as a house or a white protector are not as valuable. If a worker's residence or length of contract is uncertain, cash payments would be preferred because they allow more options.

While the shift into wage contracts especially encouraged a decline in the use of fringe benefit payments, such payments declined under both wage and tenant contracts. This was due partly to growing markets. It became more difficult for landlords to compete with chain stores and other market specialists.[6] Both landlord and tenant had an

---

[6] Rubin, op. cit., pp. 18-19.

incentive to reduce fringes. A landlord gains if he pays his work force in cash less than what it costs him to provide the fringe benefit. Similarly, a worker gains if the cash he receives allows him to purchase the identical fringe benefit and still have some cash left. It was therefore possible for both landlord and tenant to improve their status provided that specialists had sufficiently lower costs. The plantation commissary gave way to local country stores, which in turn fell to the national chain stores which offered more variety at lower prices due to economies of scale and specialization. Insurance companies and the government increasingly provided old age benefits.[7] With the increased use of automobiles and improved roads, it was no longer necessary for workers to be housed on the farm where they worked. Plantations were being transformed into "factories in the field." Workers received compensation for services performed on the farm and, at the end of the work day, left the plantation. Because landlords then had less information about the character of their employees, they were less likely to intervene in local legal disputes involving their work force. More workers turned to the Federal Government for assistance in times of need. The many New Deal programs, particularly in health and

---

[7] Rubin, *ibid.*, p. 7.

education, promoted this transition from dependence on the landlord to dependence on Uncle Sam. Where the quality and quantity of social benefits were formerly a function of playing the role of a "good Negro," they were now either purchased in the market with cash or doled out by the government. _Race-caste codes were losing their economic foundation_.

Although the landowners generally welcomed the laying aside of their former paternal burdens, whites in general scarcely appreciated what was entailed; they would now be forced to yield social concessions to blacks. Equal treatment of blacks in the consumer marketplace was one of the first concessions. Once blacks had cash, the costs to merchants of differentially treating black and white customers rose. When blacks were buying on credit advances, they were generally not served in commercial establishments until all whites had been served. With cash in their pockets, blacks were served according to the time of their arrival:

> . . . good business dictates turn-taking--both races have the same kind of money and cotton. If not satisfied at one station, the customer who has cash for gasoline goes elsewhere to buy. The man with cotton in his wagon is in a position to pay for its ginning and expects to be treated as a buyer rather than a beggar. The practice is significant because the Negro knows his place is determined by the order of his arrival rather than the color of his skin. This gives him a

taste of self-respect.[8]

Blacks with cash were now able to try on garments "rather than, as before, being required to buy shoes, gloves, hats, without first finding out whether they were the right size or shape."[9] Salesmen competing for black dollars began to address blacks as "Mr." or "Sir." Through these gestures, the independence and self-esteem of blacks was raised and was continually reinforced as they learned to handle money:

> . . . the dependent family began to acquire training in personal and family responsibility and in discriminating buying. The family seemed to take on a sense of self-direction: When furnished through a commissary, the head of the house and other members went several times a week to get this or that, each time acknowledging their dependence and usually stressing it in order to get what was wanted. When a cash allowance was given the tenant, he reported to the landlord at the first of the month to get what was his by agreement. With this money he went forth to buy where he thought he was getting the best values for his money, and where he was treated with the most consideration.[10]

With the increased independence of blacks, we observe increased tension in race relations. As work began to be divorced from social life, the cost to blacks of bucking discriminatory social mores fell. Whites at the same time

---

[8] Raper, _op_. _cit_., p. 278.

[9] Powdermaker, _op_. _cit_., p. 50.

[10] Raper, _op_. _cit_., p. 177.

were striving to retain social control but the economic lever was weakening. It is not my contention that the emergence of cash payments was necessarily the dominant reason for the observed change in race relations in the rural South between 1930 and 1960, but rather that it was a reinforcing factor (heretofore largely ignored in the literature on race relations). Many other factors outside the scope of this research were clearly significant. These include rising levels of income (which increased the amounts of cash in the hands of blacks), advancements in education, increased national exposure of Southern race relations, improvements in transportation, Federal involvement, and mechanization of the farm. The change in race relations is best viewed as a feedback process involving all of these contributing factors.

Selected Bibliography

Reports and Government Publications

Anglo-American Council on Productivity. Productivity Team Report. *Productivity in Farming*. New York: September 1951.

__________. British Farming Productivity Team. *Productivity in Farming*. London: September 1951.

Arkansas Agricultural Experiment Station. *Plantation Operations of Landlords and Tenants in Arkansas*, by H.W. Blalock. Bulletin No. 339. Fayetteville, Arkansas: May 1937.

__________. *The Farm Tenancy Situation*, by J.A. Baker and J.G. McNeely. Bulletin No. 384. Fayetteville, Arkansas: January 1940.

__________. *Changes in Labor Organization on Cotton Farms*, by J.G. McNeely and Glen T. Barton. Bulletin No. 397. Fayetteville, Arkansas: June 1940.

__________. *Income and Changes in Tenure Status of Share Renters, Share Croppers and Wage Laborers on Cotton Farms*, by J.G. McNeely, Glen T. Barton and Trimble R. Hedges. Bulletin No. 438. Fayetteville, Arkansas: June 1943.

__________. *Further Changes in Labor Used on Cotton Farms, 1939-1944*, by Otis T. Osgood and John W. White.

Bulletin No. 459. Fayetteville, Arkansas: August 1945.

Mississippi Agricultural Experiment Station. *Farm Power in the Yazoo-Mississippi Delta*, by Lewis E. Long. Bulletin No. 295. A. & M. College, Mississippi: November 1931.

Mississippi State College Agricultural Experiment Station. *Mechanical Production of Cotton*, by P.W. Gull and J.E. Adams. Bulletin No. 423. State College, Mississippi: September 1945.

__________. *Farm Mechanization in the Upland Areas of Mississippi, 1949*, by Rupert B. Johnson. Bulletin No. 502. State College, Mississippi: July 1953.

Mississippi State University Agricultural Experiment Station. *Mississippi Farm Trends, 1950-64*, by Kit Mui Leung. Bulletin No. 754. State College, Mississippi: December 1969.

__________. *Population, Growth and Redistribution in Mississippi, 1900-1970*, by Ellen S. Bryant. Bulletin No. 790. State College, Mississippi: December 1971.

South Carolina Agricultural Experiment Station. *The Farm Tenure Situation in the Southeast*, by Max M. Tharp. Bulletin No. 370. Clemson: January 1948.

__________. *Economics of Tractor Farming in the Piedmont Area of South Carolina*, by Charles P. Butler and D.E.

Crawford. Bulletin No. 377. Clemson: November 1948.

U.S. Department of Agriculture. _Yearbook of Agriculture, 1923_. "Farm Ownership and Tenancy," by L.C. Gray, O.E. Baker, F.J. Marschner, B.O. Beitz, W.R. Chapline, Ward Shepard and Raphael Zon. Washington, D.C.: Government Printing Office, 1924.

United States Department of Agriculture. _Relation of Land Tenure to Plantation Organization_, by C.O. Brannen. Bulletin No. 1269. Washington, D.C.: Government Printing Office, 1924.

__________. _The Ownership of Tenant Farms in the U.S._, by H.A. Turner. Bulletin No. 1432. Washington, D.C.: Government Printing Office, September 1926.

__________. _The Ownership of Tenant Farms in North Central States_, by H.A. Turner. Bulletin No. 1433. Washington, D.C.: Government Printing Office, September 1926.

__________. "Cotton in the Texas Plains Area," by E.A. Wooten. _Yearbook of Agriculture, 1926_. Washington, D.C.: Government Printing Office, 1926.

__________. _Plantation Organization and Operation in the Yazoo-Mississippi Delta Area_, by E.L. Langsford and B.H. Thidodeaux. Technical Bulletin No. 682. Washington, D.C.: Government Printing Office, May 1939.

__________. "Farm Wage Rates, Farm Employment and Related Data," _Agricultural Statistics, 1946_. Washington,

D.C.: Government Printing Office, 1946.

__________. *Progress of Farm Mechanization*, by Martin R. Cooper, Glen T. Barton and Albert P. Brodell. Miscellaneous Publication No. 630. Washington, D.C.: Government Printing Office, 1947.

__________. *Farm Ownership in the United States*, by Buis T. Inman and William H. Fippin. Miscellaneous Publications No. 699. Washington, D.C.: Government Printing Office, December 1949.

__________. *Analysis of Factors Influencing Cotton Yields and Their Variability*, by John L. Fulmer and Ralph R. Botts. Technical Bulletin No. 1042. Washington, D.C.: Government Printing Office, October 1951.

__________. *Yearbook of Agriculture, 1960: Power to Produce*. Washington, D.C.: Government Printing Office, 1960.

__________. *Statistics on Cotton and Related Data, 1930-1967*. Statistical Bulletin No. 417. Washington, D.C.: Government Printing Office, March 1968.

U.S. Department of Commerce. Bureau of the Census. *Fifteenth Census of the United States, 1930: Agriculture*, Special Report No. 2, The Farm Horse, by Z.R. Pettet. Washington, D.C.: Government Printing Office, 1933.

__________. Bureau of the Census. *Fifteenth Census of the United States, 1930: Agriculture*, Vol. II. Washington,

D.C.: Government Printing Office, 1932.

__________. Bureau of the Census. *Sixteenth Census of the United States, 1940: Agriculture*, Vol. I. Washington, D.C.: Government Printing Office, 1942.

__________. Bureau of the Census. *United States Census of Agriculture, 1945*, Vol. I. Washington, D.C.: Government Printing Office, 1946.

__________. Bureau of the Census. *United States Census of Agriculture: 1950*, Vol. I. Washington, D.C.: Government Printing Office, 1952.

__________. Bureau of the Census. *United States Census of Agriculture, 1954*, Vol. I. Washington, D.C.: Government Printing Office, 1956.

__________. Bureau of the Census. *United States Census of Agriculture: 1959*, Vol. I. Washington, D.C.: Government Printing Office, 1961.

__________. Bureau of the Census. *Fifteenth Census of the United States, 1930: Unemployment*, Vol. I. Washington, D.C.: Government Printing Office, 1931.

__________. Bureau of the Census. *Fifteenth Census of the United States, 1930: Population*, Vol. III. Washington, D.C.: Government Printing Office, 1932.

__________. Bureau of the Census. *Sixteenth Census of the United States, 1940: Population*, Vol. II. Washington, D.C.: Government Printing Office, 1943.

__________. Bureau of the Census. _United States Census of Population: 1950_, Vol. II. Washington, D.C.: Government Printing Office, 1952.

__________. Bureau of the Census. _United States Census of Population: 1960_, Vol. I. Washington, D.C.: Government Printing Office, 1962.

U.S. Works Progress Administration. _Landlord and Tenant on the Cotton Plantation_. Research Monograph V, Washington, D.C.: Government Printing Office, 1936.

__________. And USDA Bureau of Agricultural Economics Cooperating. _Studies of Changing Techniques and Employment in Agriculture_. Reports A9-12. Washington, D.C.: Government Printing Office, 1938.

__________. And USDA Bureau of Agricultural Economics Cooperating. _Studies of Changing Techniques and Employment in Agriculture_. Reports A13-15. Washington, D.C.: Government Printing Office, 1941.

Books and Dissertations

Blalock, Hubert M., Jr. _Social Statistics_. U.S.: McGraw-Hill, Inc., 1960.

Cheung, Steven N.S. _The Theory of Share Tenancy_. Chicago: University of Chicago Press, 1969.

Clark, Thomas D. _Three Paths to the Modern South_. Athens, Georgia: University of Georgia Press, 1965.

__________. The Emerging South. New York: Oxford University Press, 1968.

__________, ed. The South Since Reconstruction. Indianapolis, New York: The Bobbs-Merrill Company, Inc., 1973.

Cogswell, Seddie, Jr. Tenure, Nativity and Age as Factors in Iowa Agriculture, 1850-1888. Ames, Iowa: Iowa State University Press, 1975.

David, Paul. "The Mechanization of Reaping in the Ante-Bellum Midwest." Industrialization in Two Systems: Essays in Honor of Alexander Gerschenkron. Edited by Henry Rosovsky. New York: John Wiley and Sons, 1966.

Davis, Allison, Burleigh B. Gardner and Mary R. Gardner. Deep South. Chicago: University of Chicago Press, 1941.

Ferber, Robert. Market Research. U.S.: McGraw-Hill, Inc., 1949.

Fulmer, John L. Agricultural Progress in the Cotton Belt since 1920. Chapel Hill: The University of North Carolina Press, 1950.

Gray, L.C. Introduction to Agricultural Economics. New York: MacMillan, 1924.

Groh, George W. The Black Migration. New York: Weybright and Talley, 1972.

Higgs, Robert. Competition and Coercion. New York:

Cambridge University Press, 1977.

Hoffsommer, Harold, ed. *The Social and Economic Significance of Land Tenure in the Southwestern States*. Chapel Hill: University of North Carolina Press, 1950.

Johnson, Charles S., Edwin R. Embree and W.W. Alexander. *The Collapse of Cotton Tenancy*. Chapel Hill: University of North Carolina Press, 1935.

Johnson, Charles S. *Shadow of the Plantation*. Chicago: University of Chicago Press, 1966.

Martin, Lee R., ed. *A Survey of Agricultural Economics Literature*, Vol. 1. Minneapolis: University of Minnesota Press, 1977.

McGregor, Alexander C. "The Agricultural Development of the Columbia Plateau: McGregor Land and Livestock Company, A Case History." Unpublished Ph.D. dissertation, University of Washington, 1977.

Moody, Anne. *Coming of Age in Mississippi*. New York: The Dial Press, 1968.

Musoka, Moses S. "Technical Change in Cotton Production in the U.S., 1935-1960." Unpublished Ph.D. dissertation, University of Wisconsin-Madison, 1976.

Myrdal, Gunnar. *An American Dilemma*. New York: McGraw-Hill, 1964.

Nicholls, William H. *Southern Tradition and Regional Progress*. Chapel Hill: University of North Carolina

Press, 1960.

North, Douglass C. and Robert P. Thomas. The Rise of the Western World. New York: Cambridge University Press, 1973.

Percy, William Alexander. Lanterns on the Levee. New York: Alfred A. Knopf, 1941.

Powdermaker, Hortense. After Freedom. New York: Atheneum, 1968.

Rao, Putluri and Roger LeRoy Miller. Applied Econometrics. Belmont, California: Wadsworth Publishing Co., 1971.

Raper, Arthur F. Preface to Peasantry. New York: Atheneum, 1968.

__________. Tenants of the Almighty. New York: The MacMillan Company, 1943.

Rosengarten, Theodore. All God's Dangers: The Life of Nate Shaw. New York: Avon Books, 1974.

Rubin, Morton. Plantation County. Chapel Hill: University of North Carolina Press, 1951.

Scheffé, Henry. The Analysis of Variance. New York: John Wiley & Sons, Inc., 1959.

Stone, Alfred H. Studies in the American Race Problem. New York: Doubleday, Page and Company, 1908.

Street, James H. The New Revolution in the Cotton Economy. Chapel Hill: University of North Carolina Press, 1957.

Tang, Anthony M. Economic Development in the Southern Piedmont, 1860-1950. Chapel Hill: University of North

Carolina Press, 1958.

Vance, Rupert B. Human Geography of the South. New York: Russell and Russell, 1968.

Articles in Periodicals and Books

Alchian, Armen, Robert G. Crawford and Benjamin Klein. "Ownership Specialization and Asset Integration in the Firm." Preliminary unpublished manuscript, UCLA, May 1977.

Bardhan, P.K. and T.N. Srinivason. "Cropsharing Tenancy in Agriculture: A Theoretical and Empirical Analysis." American Economic Review, LXI (March 1971), 48-64.

__________. "Cropsharing Tenancy in Agriculture: Rejoinder." American Economic Review, LXIV (December 1974), 1067-1069.

Cheung, Steven N.S. "Transactions Costs, Risk Aversion, and the Choice of Contractual Arrangements." Journal of Law and Economics, XII (April 1969), 23-42.

David, Paul. "A Contribution to the Theory of Diffusion." Memorandum No. 71. Stanford University (June 1969).

Day, R.H. "Technological Change and the Sharecropper." American Economic Review, LVII (June 1967), 427-449.

Epstein, T. Scarlett. "The Ideal Marriage between the Economist's Macro Approach and the Social Anthropologist's Micro Approach to Development Studies."

Economic Development and Cultural Change (April 1976), 29-45.

Fenoaltea, Stefano. "The Rise and Fall of a Theoretical Model: The Manorial System." Journal of Economic History, XXXV (June 1975), 386-409.

__________. "Authority, Efficiency, and Agricultural Organization in Medieval England and Beyond: A Hypothesis." Journal of Economic History, XXXV (December 1975), 693-718.

__________. "Risk, Transactions Costs, and the Organization of Medieval Agriculture." Explorations in Economic History, 13 (April 1976), 129-151.

Flesig, Heywood. "Mechanizing the Cotton Harvest in the Nineteenth-Century South." Journal of Economic History, XXX (December 1965), 704-706.

Griliches, Zvi. "The Demand for a Durable Input: Farm Tractors in the United States, 1921-57," The Demand for Durable Goods. Edited by Arnold C. Harberger. Chicago: University of Chicago Press, 1960.

Higgs, Robert. "Race, Tenure, and Resource Allocation in Southern Agriculture, 1910." Journal of Economic History, XXXIII (March 1973), 146-169.

__________. "Patterns of Farm Rental in the Georgia Cotton Belt, 1880-1900." Journal of Economic History, XXXIV (June 1974), 468-482.

__________. "Tractors or Horses? Some Basic Economics in the Pacific Northwest and Elsewhere." Agricultural History, XLIX (January 1975), 281-283.

__________. "The Boll Weevil, the Cotton Economy and Black Migration, 1910-1930." Agricultural History, 50 (April 1976), 335-350.

__________. "Competing Interpretations of Contractual Arrangements in Agriculture: A Note on the Evidence, with a New Look at the Boll Weevil." Discussion Paper No. 77-5. University of Washington (April 1977).

Jones, Lewis R. "The Mechanization of Reaping and Mowing in American Agriculture, 1833-1870: Comment." Journal of Economic History, XXXVII (June 1977), 451-455.

McGuire, Robert and Robert Higgs. "Cotton, Corn and Risk in the Nineteenth Century: Another View." Explorations in Economic History, 14 (April 1977), 167-182.

McCloskey, Donald N. "Fenoaltea on Open Fields: A Comment." Explorations in Economic History, 14 (October 1977), 402-404.

Newberry, D.M.G. "Cropsharing Tenancy in Agriculture: A Theoretical and Empirical Analysis: Comment." American Economic Review, LXIV (December 1974), 1060-1066.

__________. "Sharecropping and Uncertain Labor Markets." Review of Economic Studies, 44 (October 1977), 585-594.

Nicholls, William H. "The Effects of Industrial Development on Tennessee Valley Agriculture, 1900-1950." Journal of Farm Economics, XXXVIII (December 1956), 1636-1649.

__________. "Industrial-Urban Development and Agricultural Adjustments, Tennessee Valley and Piedmont, 1939-1954." Journal of Political Economy, LXVIII (April 1960), 135-149.

North, Douglass C. and Robert P. Thomas. "The Rise and Fall of the Manorial System: A Theoretical Model." Journal of Economic History, XXXI (December 1971), 779-803.

Olmstead, Alan L. "The Mechanization of Reaping and Mowing in American Agriculture, 1833-1878." Journal of Economic History, XXXV (June 1975), 327-352.

Pederson, Harold A. and Arthur F. Raper. "Changes in Mississippi Cotton Plantations." Agriculture in the United States, Vol. III. Edited by Wayne D. Rasmussen. New York: Random House, 1975.

Peterson, Willis and Yujiro Hayami. "Technical Change in Agriculture." Agricultural Economics Literature, Vol. I. Edited by Lee R. Martin. Minneapolis: University of Minnesota Press, 1972.

Rasmussen, Wayne. "The Impact of Technological Change on American Agriculture, 1862-1962." Journal of Economic History, XXII (December 1962), 578-591.

Reid, Joseph D., Jr. "Sharecropping as an Understandable

Market Response: The Post-Bellum South." Journal of Economic History, XXXIII (March 1973), 106-130.

__________. "Ante-Bellum Southern Rental Contracts." Explorations in Economic History, XIII (January 1976), 69-83.

__________. "Notes Toward a Geography of Farm Tenure Choice." Unpublished, University of Chicago.

__________. "The Theory of Share Tenancy Revisited--Again." Journal of Political Economy, LXXXV (April 1977), 403-407.

__________. "Sharecropping and Tenancy in American History." Risk and Uncertainty in Agriculture. Edited by James Roumasset. Forthcoming. Berkeley, California: University of California Press.

Stiglitz, Joseph E. "Incentives and Risk Sharing in Sharecropping." Review of Economic Studies, 61 (April 1974), 219-256.

Winters, D.L. "Tenant Farming in Iowa, 1860-1900: A Study of the Terms of Rental Leases." Agricultural History, XLVIII (January 1974), 130-150.

Wright, G. and H. Kunreuther. "Cotton, Corn and Risk in the Nineteenth Century." Journal of Economic History, XXXV (September 1975), 526-551.

__________. "Cotton, Corn and Risk in the Nineteenth Century: A Reply." Explorations in Economic History,

14 (April 1977), 183-195.

Appendix A

Data Sources and Sample Counties

Sources for the data include the *United States Census of Agriculture* for 1930, 1940, 1945, 1950, 1954 and 1959, the Fifteenth, Sixteenth (1950 and 1960) *Census of the U.S.* and *Historical Statistics of the U.S.*, which is the source for the wage deflator. The data necessary to generate the urbanization and employment variables are contained in the *Population Censuses of the U.S.*, except for the observations on employment for 1930, which are in the *Unemployment Census of the U.S.: 1930*. All the data for the remaining variables are in the *U.S. Censuses of Agriculture*. Table 5 lists the volumes and county tables (C.T.) from which the data set was collected.

The ten cotton producing states included in my study, North Carolina, South Carolina, Georgia, Tennessee, Alabama, Mississippi, Louisiana, Arkansas, Oklahoma and Texas, contain 1023 counties. Because of the costs entailed with collecting observations from every county for six census years, I instead collected a random sample of twenty-five observations from each state. The sample counties selected are shaded in Figures 3-12.

Table 5

Data Sources

	1930	1940	1945	1950	1955	1960
Census of Agriculture	Vol. II Part 2	Vol. I Parts 3-5	Vol. I Parts 16, 17, 20-26	Vol. I Parts 16, 17, 20-26	Vol. I (1954) Parts 16, 17, 20-26	Vol. I (1959) Parts 26-28, 31-37
Tenants	C.T. 1	C.T. 2	C.T. 5	C.T. 2a	C.T. 2	C.T. 3
Wages	C.T. 12	C.T. 10	C.T. 1	C.T. 3	C.T. 6	C.T. 7
Total Cropland H.	C.T. 1	C.T. 1	C.T. 1	C.T. 1	C.T. 1	C.T. 1
Cotton Acreage	C.T. 5	C.T. 7	C.T. 2	C.T. 5	C.T. 9	C.T. 11
Corn Acreage	C.T. 5	C.T. 6	C.T. 2	C.T. 5	C.T. 9	C.T. 11
Legume Acreage	C.T. 7	C.T. 12	C.T. 2	C.T. 5	C.T. 9	C.T. 11
Cotton Bales	C.T. 5	C.T. 7	C.T. 2	C.T. 5	C.T. 9	C.T. 11
Tractors	C.T. 12	C.T. 10	C.T. 1	C.T. 3	C.T. 5	C.T. 6
Horses	C.T. 4	C.T. 4	C.T. 3	C.T. 4	C.T. 7	C.T. 8
Mules	C.T. 4	C.T. 4	C.T. 3	C.T. 4	C.T. 7	C.T. 8
Historical Statistics	Part 1	Part 1	Part 1	Part 1	Part 1	Part 1
Wage Deflator	Series K 344-353	Series K 344-353	Series K 344-353	Series K 344-353	Series K 344-353	Series K 344-353
Population Census	Vol. III Parts 1 and 2	Vol. II Parts 1-6		Vol. II Parts 2, 4, 11, 18, 24, 33, 36, 40, 42 and 43		Vol. I Parts 2, 5, 12, 20, 26, 35, 38, 42, 44 and 45

Table 5. Data Sources (continued)

	1930	1940	1945	1950	1955	1960
Population Census (continued)						
Total Population	Table 13	Table 21		Table 42		Table 82
Urban Population	Table 13					
Labor Force		Table 23		Table 43		Table 83
Employed		Table 23		Table 43		Table 83
Rural Farm Population		Table 21		Table 49		}Table 91
Rural Nonfarm Population		Table 26		Table 48		
Unemployment Census	Vol. 1					
Labor Force	Table 10					
Class A-UE	Table 10					
Class B-UE	Table 10					

Figure 3. Sample Counties--North Carolina.

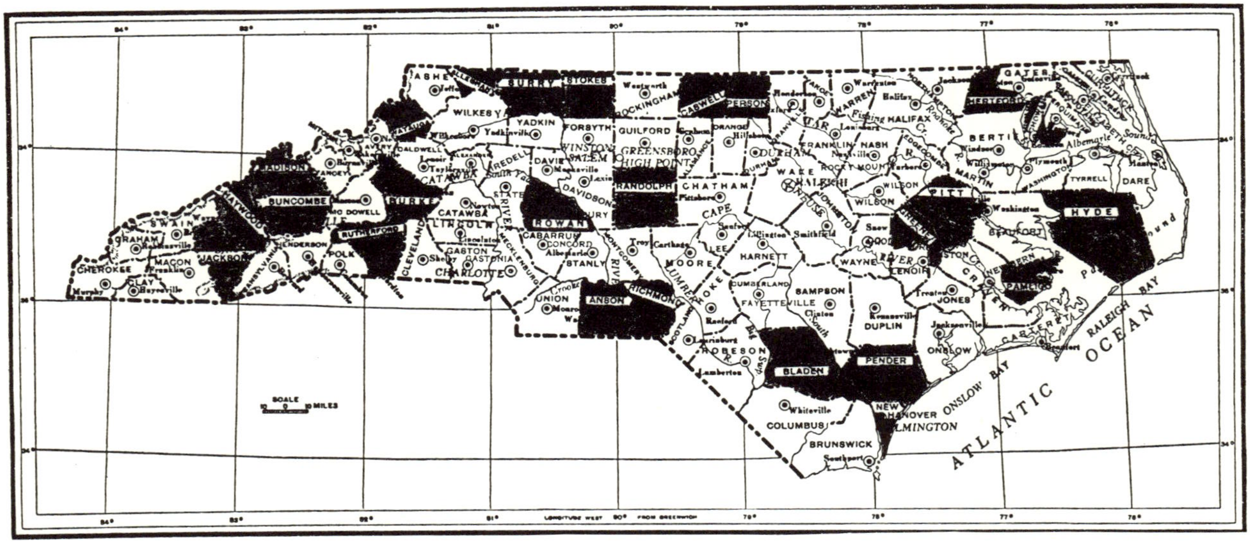

Figure 4. Sample Counties--North Carolina.

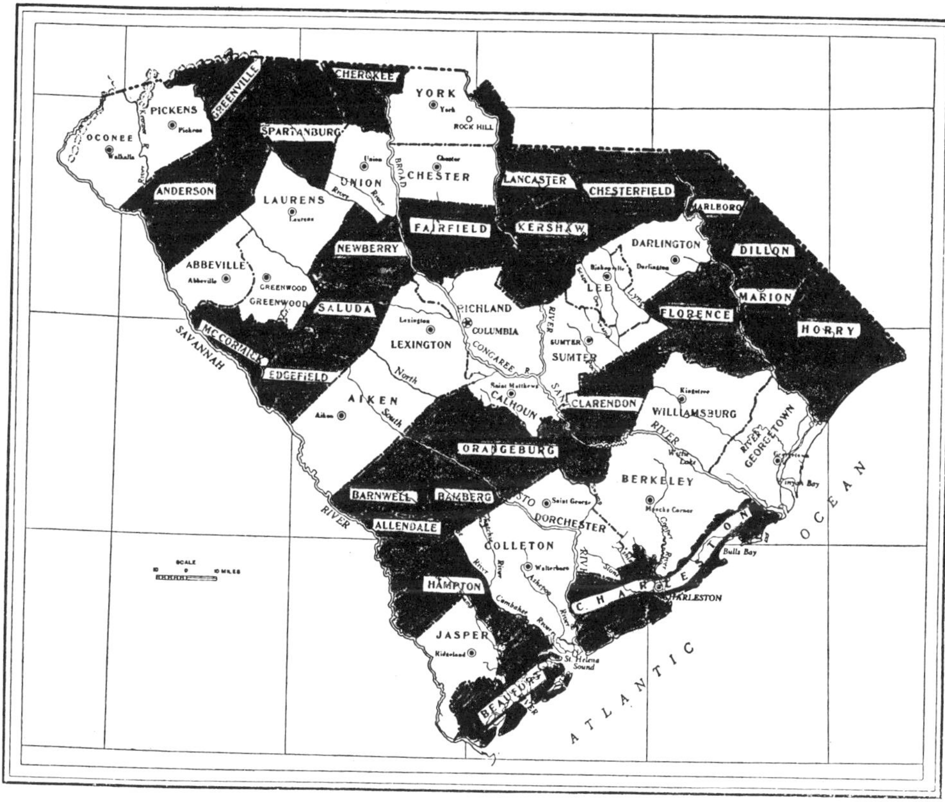

Figure 5. Sample Counties--Georgia.

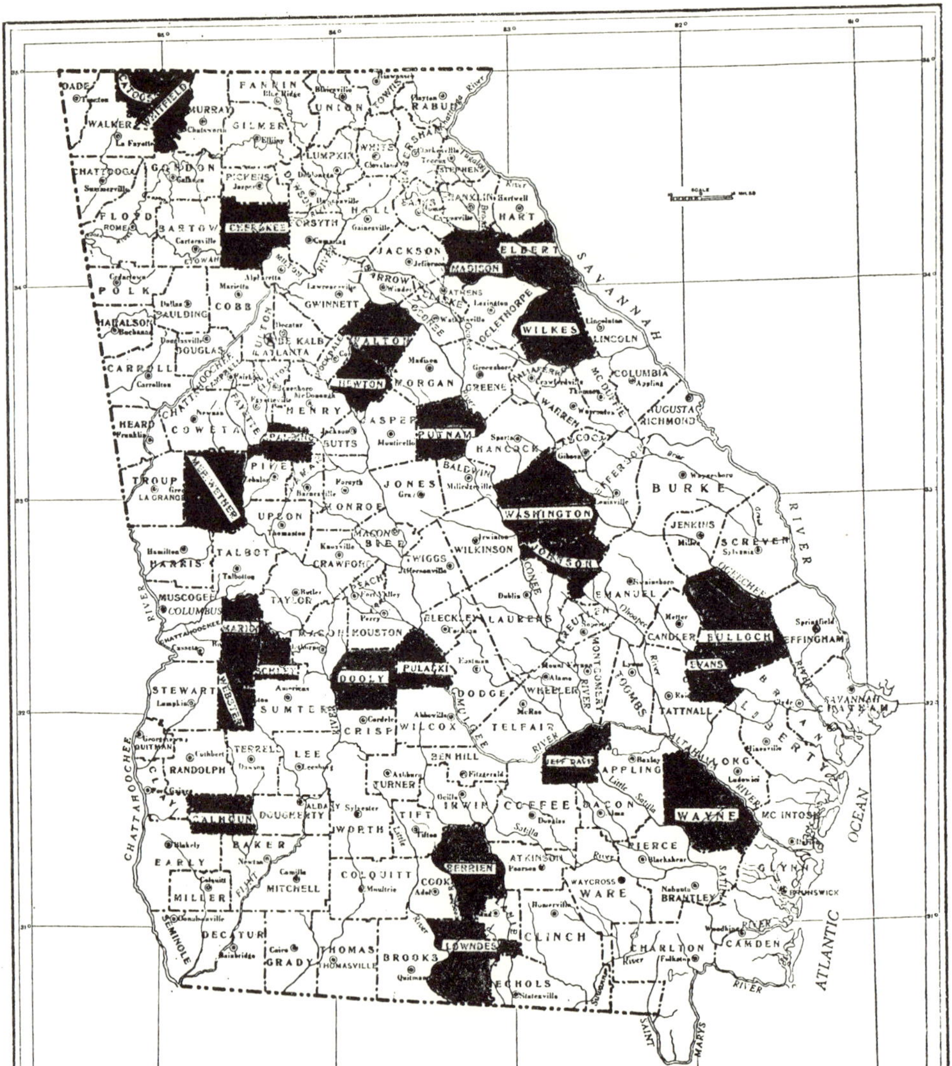

Figure 6. Sample Counties--Tennessee.

Figure 7. Sample Counties--Alabama.

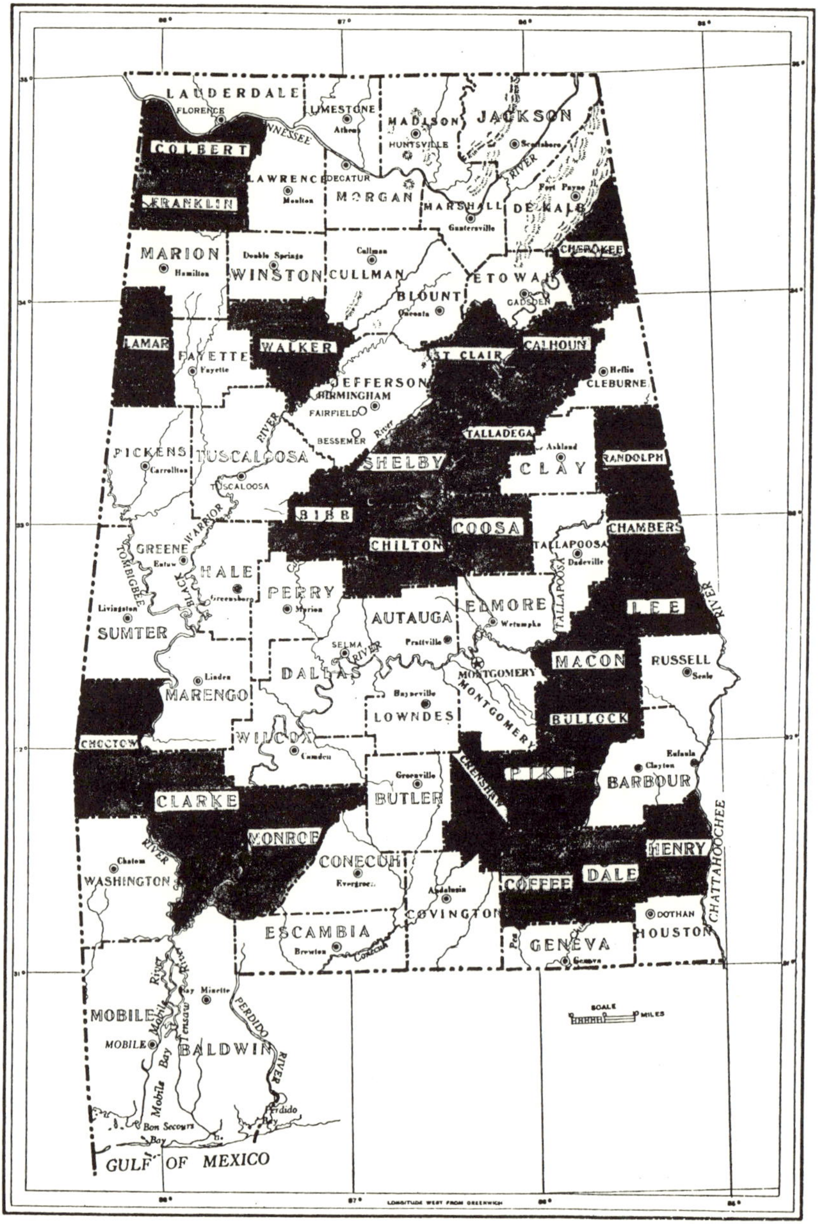

Figure 8. Sample Counties--Mississippi

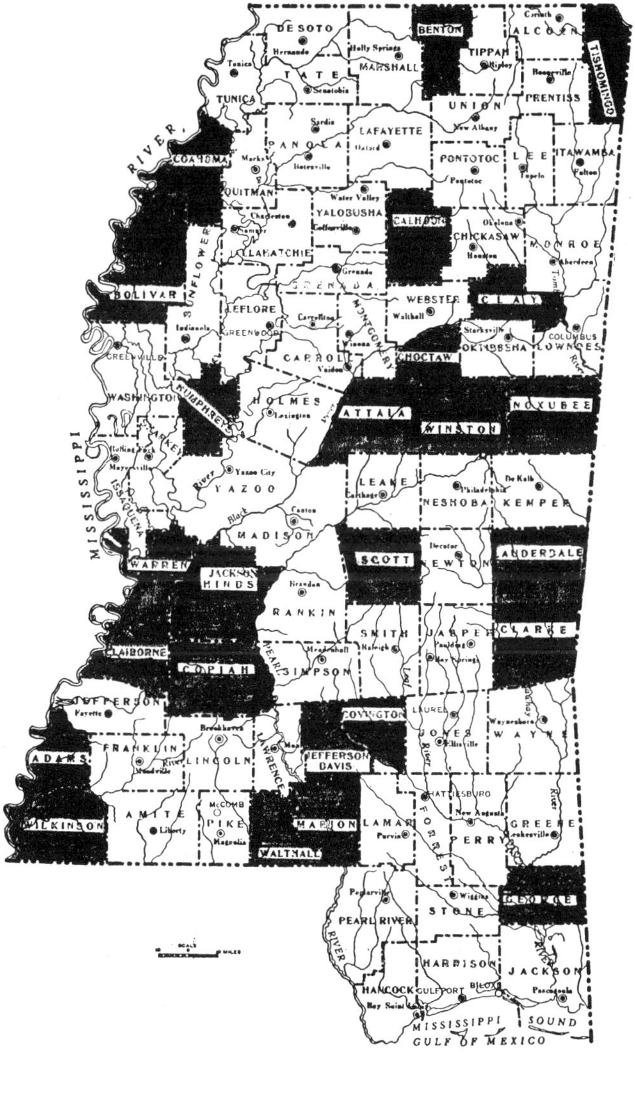

Figure 9. Sample Counties--Arkansas.

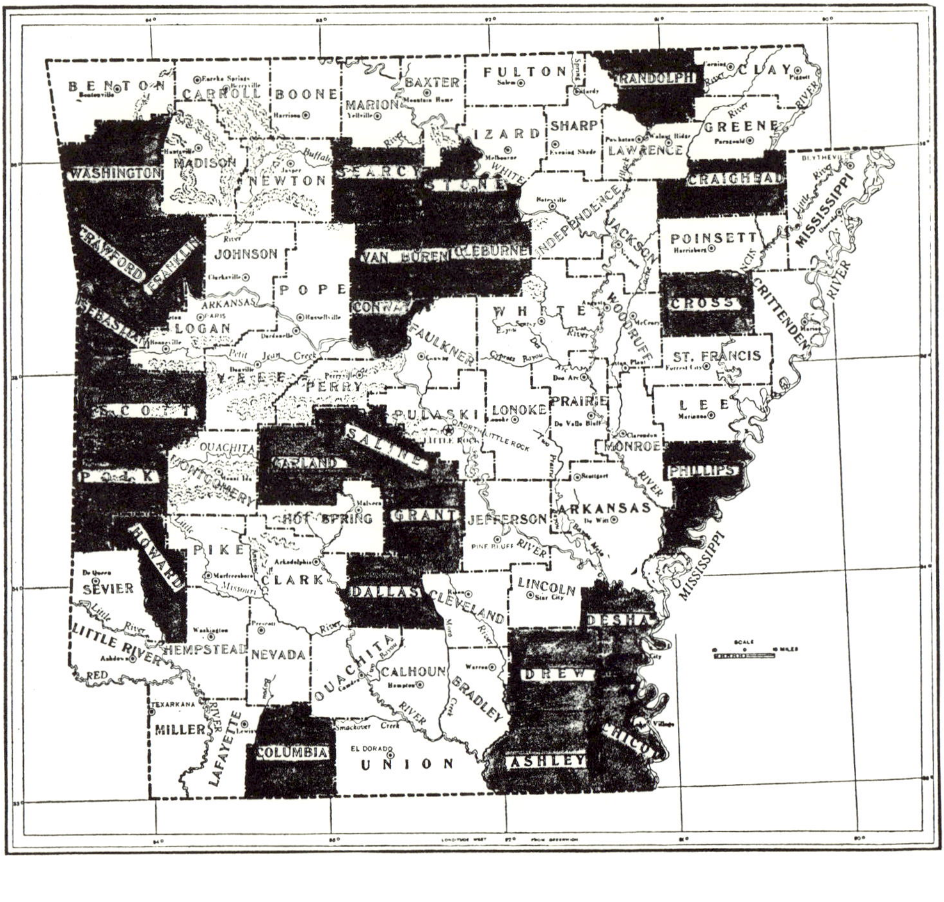

Figure 10. Sample Counties--Louisiana.

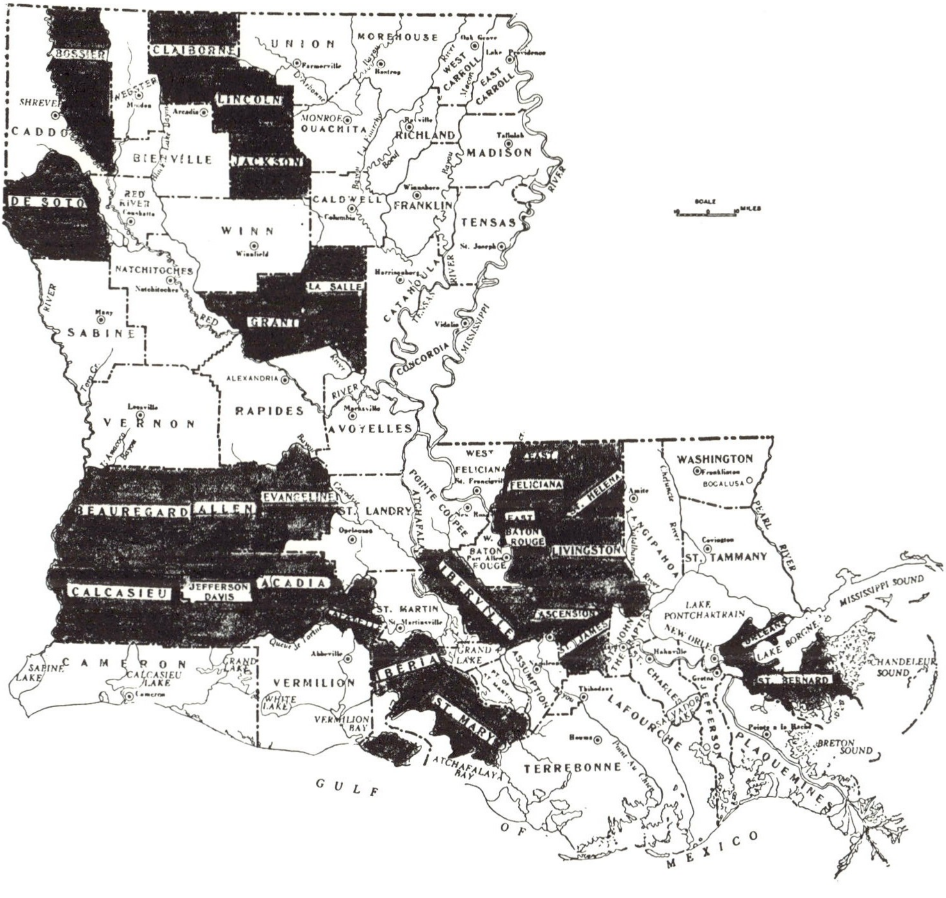

Figure 11. Sample Counties--Oklahoma.

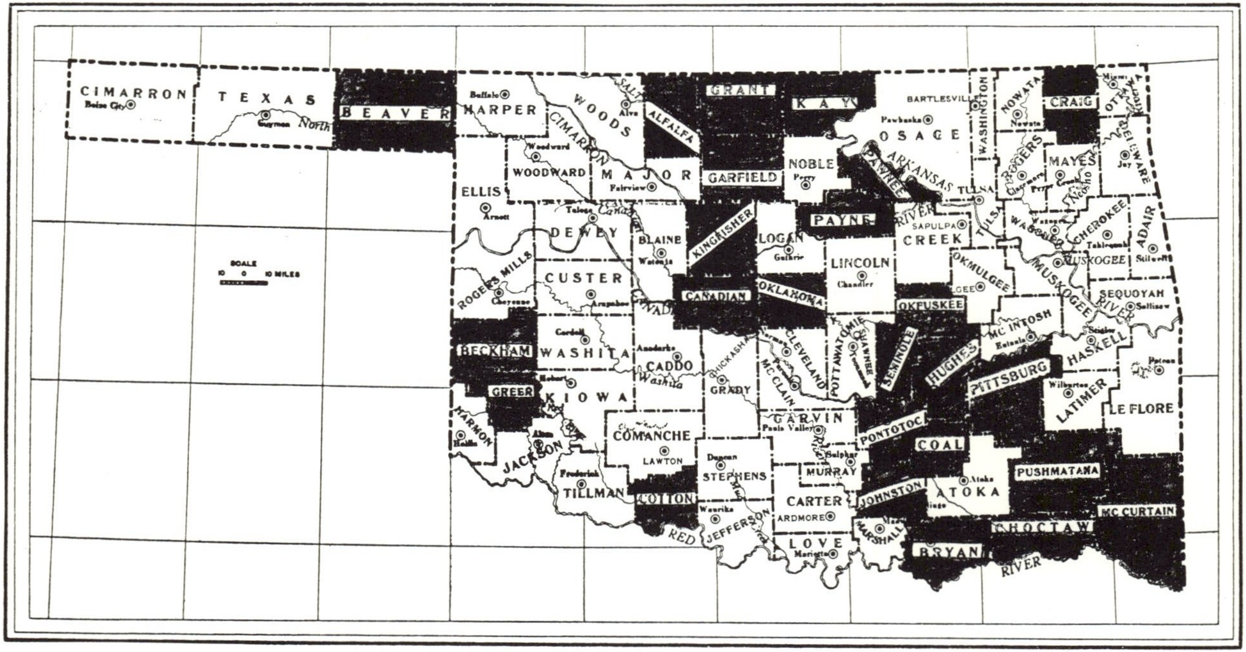

Figure 12. Sample Counties--Texas.

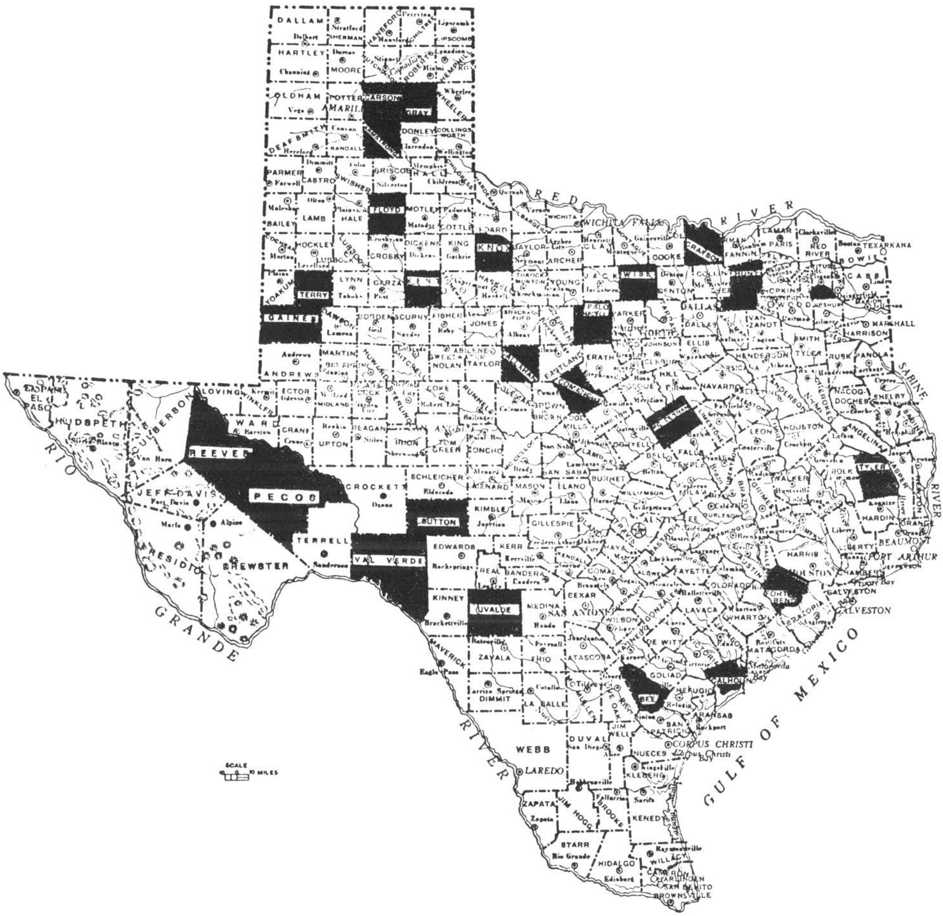